PO 22669   Dawson   005.369   £16.99 ✓

ECDL
Connect

P.K. McBride

Heinemann Educational Publishers
Halley Court, Jordan Hill, Oxford OX2 8EJ
Part of Harcourt Education

Heinemann is the registered trademark of
Harcourt Education Limited

© text P.K. McBride, 2005

First published 2005

10 09 08 07 06 05
10 9 8 7 6 5 4 3 2 1

British Library Cataloguing in Publication Data is available
from the British Library on request.

ISBN 0 435 44978 8

 Typeset by P.K. McBride, Southampton

Cover design by Wooden Ark Studio

Printed in the UK by Scotprint Ltd

Cover photo: © Digital Vision

Acknowledgements
Every effort has been made to contact copyright holders of material reproduced in this
book. Any omissions will be rectified in subsequent printings if notice is given to the
publishers.

Websites
Please note that the examples of websites suggested in this book were up to date at the
time of writing. It is essential for tutors to preview each site before using it to ensure that
the URL is still accurate and the content is appropriate. We suggest that tutors bookmark
useful sites and consider enabling students to access them through the school or college
intranet.

Screenshots reprinted with permission from Microsoft Corporation.

Contents

Module 7: Information and communication 153

The Resource Bank contains:

• assignment papers and source files for all modules

• source files for Skill Builders in:

   Module 2: Using the computer and managing files

   Module 3: Word processing

   Module 4: Spreadsheets

   Module 5: Databases

   Module 6: Presentations

Introduction

This book and its accompanying CD are designed to be used alongside the Electric Paper e-tutor. The book acts as a guide to the computer-based learning and provides extra practice material along with summaries, tips and reminders. The **Skill Builders** should be completed immediately after the related part of the e-tutor as they give practice in the aspects that have just been covered. Some of these use files which can be found on the CD. The CD also contains additional **assignments** to consolidate techniques and concepts.

This book does not cover *Concepts of Information Technology*, as that module has no practical components.

The book and the e-tutor

At the top of most pages in the book is a menu display which allows you to see at a glance which modules and sections of the e-tutor you are working through.

The items highlighted in **bold red** are the ones which relate to the page. Work your way through them before returning to the page and attempting the relevant Skill Builder.

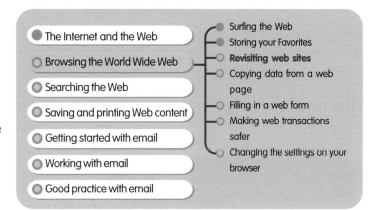

Which Windows? Which Office?

There are currently six versions of Microsoft Windows and three versions of Microsoft Office in general use. This book has been written around Windows XP and Office XP (2002/2003). The screen displays, toolbars and menu systems shown here can be found with very slight variations in Windows 98, Me, NT and 2000, and in Office 2000. Where the differences may be enough to cause any confusion, they are pointed out. Look out for these boxes.

> In Word 2000 **File > New** opens the **New** dialogue box. The **Blank document** option is on the **General** tab.
>
> In Word 2002/2003 **File > New** opens the **New document** task pane. The **Blank document** option is in the **New** section.

There are two editions of Office XP currently in use – the original 2002 and the updated 2003. The differences are very slight, and do not affect anything at the level of this book.

Fonts and styles

Menu items, labels on buttons, headings and other key words on the screen are shown in **bold**, e.g. the **File** menu, the **OK** button.

Names of files, folders and fields in worksheets are shown in *italics*, e.g. the *tes.doc* file, *My Documents* folder.

Anything which you are asked to type is shown in Times New Roman, e.g. type the heading Deleting and replacing.

Keys are identified by [brackets], e.g. **[Insert]**. Where two or more keys must be pressed, they are linked by a + sign, e.g. **[Alt] + [F]** means hold down the **[Alt]** key and press **[F]**.

Menu commands may be presented in a short form, with > indicating the steps through the menu, e.g. 'open the **File** menu and select **Print**' may be written as 'use **File > Print**'.

Tips and warnings

Watch out for boxes like these:

 This is a tip – try to remember it as it could make your life easier.

 This is a warning – if you get this wrong, it could harm your files or your PC, or your chances in the ECDL assessments.

The Resource Bank

This book is also accompanied by a Resource Bank – a CD-ROM containing the source files that are needed in the assignments and Skill Builders. The files should be copied into a convenient area of your computer or network at the start of the course, so that they can be accessed more easily when they are needed.

Assignments

The Resource Bank also contains two or three assignments for each unit. These are in PDF form, and can be printed as needed. When you see one of these boxes, you know it's time for the next assignment.

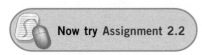 **Now try Assignment 2.2**

Module 2

USING THE COMPUTER AND MANAGING FILES

Computer systems come in a wide range of shapes and sizes, from room-sized **mainframes** down to pocket-sized **handhelds**. They are designed for an ever-widening range of purposes, from managing the accounts of global organisations to controlling production-line robots.

In the ECDL course, and in this book, the focus is on the PC (personal computer) – either a desktop or laptop model – running some form of Windows. For the last ten years, and for the foreseeable future, these have been and will be the standard computers – the ones that you will see on the desks in any office and in homes.

- ○ Using the computer and managing files
- ○ Word processing
- ○ Spreadsheets
- ○ Databases
- ○ Presentations
- ○ Information and communication

 Throughout this unit you will be asked to open files that are supplied in the Resource Bank. They can be found on the Resource Bank CD or in the folder which your tutor may have set up for use with this course.

Looking at the Desktop

Starting your computer

The Desktop is at the heart of Windows. The one below is Windows 98, but NT, 2000 and XP all have the same components. You can customise the colour scheme, fonts, background and other features, so desktops vary hugely.

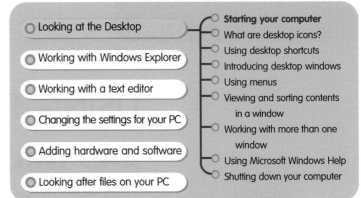

- Looking at the Desktop
- Working with Windows Explorer
- Working with a text editor
- Changing the settings for your PC
- Adding hardware and software
- Looking after files on your PC

- **Starting your computer**
- What are desktop icons?
- Using desktop shortcuts
- Introducing desktop windows
- Using menus
- Viewing and sorting contents in a window
- Working with more than one window
- Using Microsoft Windows Help
- Shutting down your computer

Shortcut icons

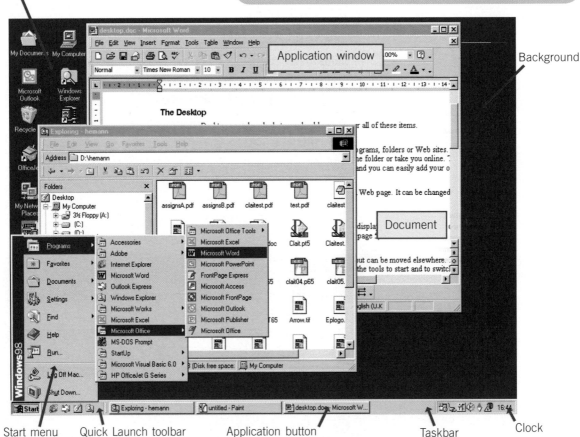

Application window

Background

Document

Start menu   Quick Launch toolbar   Application button   Taskbar   Clock

Skill Builder 2.1

1   Switch on your PC and its monitor and wait for the PC to start up.

2   If you are on a network, type your username and password to logon.

3   Explore your desktop.

Icons and windows

Windows have three display modes: Maximized, Minimized and Restore.

When a window is in Restore mode, you can move or resize it. The simplest way to do this is by 'dragging'. To drag, keep the left button down while you move the mouse. When you release the button, the object will drop into its new place.

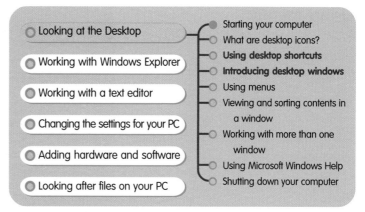

- Looking at the Desktop
  - Starting your computer
  - What are desktop icons?
  - **Using desktop shortcuts**
  - **Introducing desktop windows**
  - Using menus
  - Viewing and sorting contents in a window
  - Working with more than one window
  - Using Microsoft Windows Help
  - Shutting down your computer
- Working with Windows Explorer
- Working with a text editor
- Changing the settings for your PC
- Adding hardware and software
- Looking after files on your PC

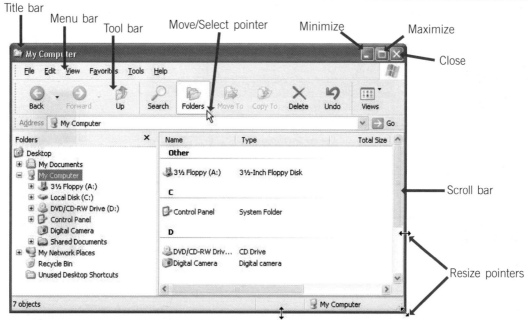

Title bar · Menu bar · Tool bar · Move/Select pointer · Minimize · Maximize · Close · Scroll bar · Resize pointers

Skill Builder 2.2

1 Locate the *My Computer* icon on the desktop or its entry in the **Start** menu.

2 Double-click on the icon or the name. A window will open, showing the disk drives and other main areas of the PC.

3 Switch the window into **Maximize** and then into **Restore** mode.

4 Click on the Title bar of the *My Computer* window. Keeping the mouse button down, move the mouse to drag the window across the screen.

5 Drop the window into a new position.

6 Move the mouse over an edge of the window frame to get the double-arrow, then drag the edge to change the size of the window.

Using menus

In any application, the full range of its commands and facilities can be reached through the menu bar.

You can often open a context or shortcut menu by right-clicking on an object. This has a selection of commands that relate to that object.

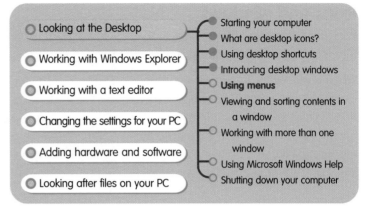

- ● Looking at the Desktop
- ● Working with Windows Explorer
- ● Working with a text editor
- ● Changing the settings for your PC
- ● Adding hardware and software
- ● Looking after files on your PC

- ● Starting your computer
- ● What are desktop icons?
- ● Using desktop shortcuts
- ● Introducing desktop windows
- ○ **Using menus**
- ○ Viewing and sorting contents in a window
- ○ Working with more than one window
- ○ Using Microsoft Windows Help
- ○ Shutting down your computer

Using a menu opened from the Menu bar

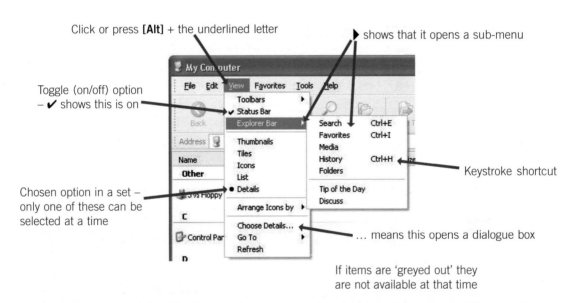

Click or press **[Alt]** + the underlined letter

shows that it opens a sub-menu

Toggle (on/off) option – ✔ shows this is on

Chosen option in a set – only one of these can be selected at a time

Keystroke shortcut

… means this opens a dialogue box

If items are 'greyed out' they are not available at that time

---

Skill Builder **2.3**

1 If *My Computer* is not already open, double-click on its desktop icon to run it.

2 Use the mouse to open the **View** menu.

3 Click on the **Status Bar** item – what happens?

4 Open the **View** menu again – this time use the keyboard.

5 Move slowly down through the items. If a sub-menu opens, look at its options to see what is there.

Viewing and sorting contents in a window

My Computer shows you the files and folders on your PC. You can view them in several ways and arrange the icons in different orders.

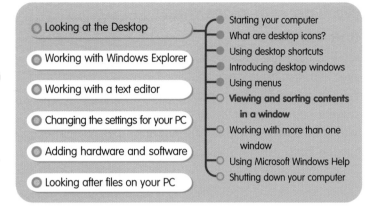

- Looking at the Desktop
- Working with Windows Explorer
- Working with a text editor
- Changing the settings for your PC
- Adding hardware and software
- Looking after files on your PC

- Starting your computer
- What are desktop icons?
- Using desktop shortcuts
- Introducing desktop windows
- Using menus
- **Viewing and sorting contents in a window**
- Working with more than one window
- Using Microsoft Windows Help
- Shutting down your computer

Skill Builder 2.4

1 In *My Computer*, double-click on the C: drive icon. (This may open another window – carry on working in the new window.)

2 Open the **View** menu.

3 Click on each of the items from **Large Icons** down to **Details** – how does the display change? (In Windows XP you also have a **Thumbnails** option.)

4 Open the **View** menu, then the **Arrange Icons by** sub-menu. Select **Modified** to arrange the icons in date order.

5 Use the **Arrange Icons by** sub-menu to put the files in **Name** order.

6 Switch the view to **Details**.

7 Click on the headings at the top of the columns. What happens? What happens if you click twice on the same heading?

Change the display with the **View** commands

Click on a heading to sort files by that column

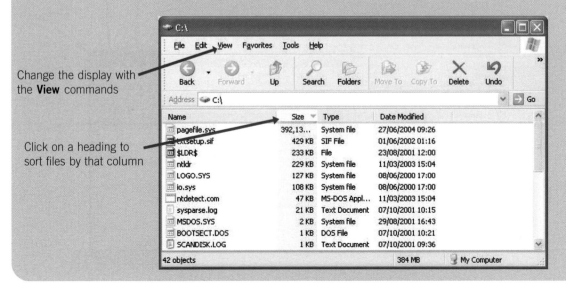

Working with more than one window

You can have several windows open at once, and can move easily between them using the Taskbar buttons. If the active window does not fill the screen, you can click on another window to bring it to the front.

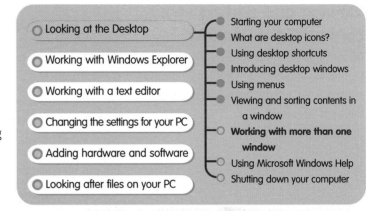

- Looking at the Desktop
  - Starting your computer
  - What are desktop icons?
  - Using desktop shortcuts
  - Introducing desktop windows
- Working with Windows Explorer
  - Using menus
  - Viewing and sorting contents in a window
- Working with a text editor
- Changing the settings for your PC
  - **Working with more than one window**
- Adding hardware and software
  - Using Microsoft Windows Help
  - Shutting down your computer
- Looking after files on your PC

Skill Builder 2.5

1 Open *My Computer*, the *Recycle Bin* and another program by double-clicking on their Desktop icons.

2 Drag on the Title bars so that the windows overlap.

3 Click on any visible part of an underlying window to make it active.

4 Set the current window to Maximized.

5 Use the Taskbar to make one of the hidden windows active.

6 Close all three windows by clicking on their **Close** buttons.

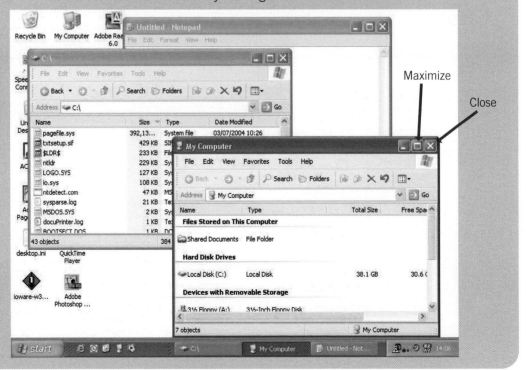

Using Microsoft Windows Help

There's always Help at hand in Windows. The Help systems look different in Windows XP and 98/Me, but they work in the same way.

Windows 98 Help

Click on the book icons to display the contents

Search for Help

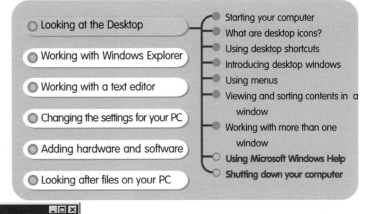

Click on blue underlined text to go to its linked Help page

Windows XP Help

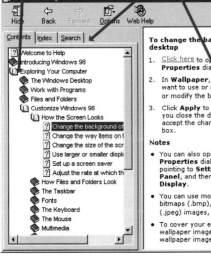

➕ indicates a folder – click to display its topics

Select a heading at the opening page, then pick a topic

Skill Builder **2.6**

1 Open the **Start** menu and select **Help** (**Help and Support** in XP).

2 Browse through Help, and try to find Help on customising the desktop.

3 Try a search. Go to the **Search** routine and type in 'desktop background'.

4 Select a topic from the list that is offered to you.

5 When you have finished, exit from Help by clicking on its **Close** button.

6 On the **Start** menu, select **Shut Down** (**Turn Off Computer** in Windows XP) and confirm this at the prompt.

Working with Windows Explorer

Windows Explorer

Windows Explorer is opened from the Start menu. It is a variation of *My Computer*, the main difference being the two-pane display, with the folder list on the left and the contents of the selected folder on the right.

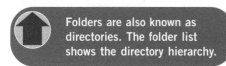 Folders are also known as directories. The folder list shows the directory hierarchy.

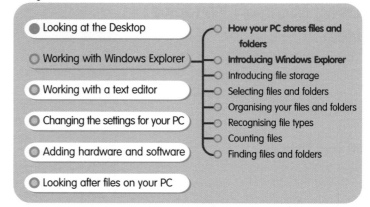

Change the View

The name of the current folder is shown in the **Title bar**

Click a folder name to display its contents

Click to close the subfolders

Click to open its subfolders

If the Status bar is not visible, open the **View** menu and click **Status bar** to turn it on

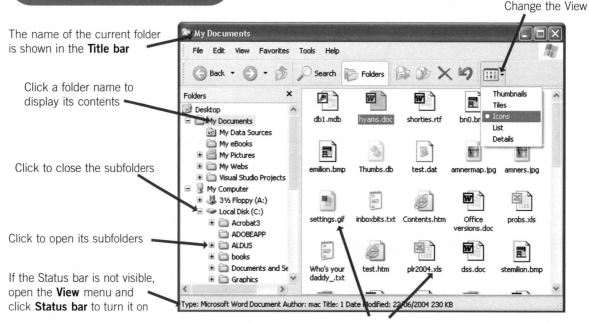

The extension after the name may not be shown – see page 13

Skill Builder **2.7**

1 Open Windows Explorer from the **Start** menu.

2 If the Folder pane is not present, click the **Folders** in the toolbar (in Windows 98/Me open the **View** menu, point to **Explorer Bar** and tick **Folders**).

3 Click on a folder to display its contents.

4 Use the **View** menu or **View** button to change the display style.

5 Click ⊞ beside **Local Disk (C:)** to show its folders.

6 Click ⊞ beside any folder to show its subfolders.

Introducing file storage

Formatting a floppy disk

You will need a floppy disk in later exercises, so now would be a good time to prepare one. You need a new floppy disk, or one that only contains files that no-one wants.

- Looking at the Desktop
- Working with Windows Explorer
- Working with a text editor
- Changing the settings for your PC
- Adding hardware and software
- Looking after files on your PC

- How your PC stores files and folders
- Introducing Windows Explorer
- **Introducing file storage**
- Selecting files and folders
- Organising your files and folders
- Recognising file types
- Counting files
- Finding files and folders

Skill Builder **2.8**

1 Place the floppy disk in the drive.

2 Go to Windows Explorer. Select **3½ Floppy Drive** and see what files, if any, are on it. Can they be deleted?

3 Right-click on **3½ Floppy Drive** and select **Format...**

4 At the **Format 3½ Floppy** dialogue box, turn on the **Quick Format** option, then click **Start**.

5 You will be warned that formatting will erase any files. Click **OK**.

6 When the formatting is complete, click **OK** when you've read the message, then **Close** to close the **Format** dialogue box.

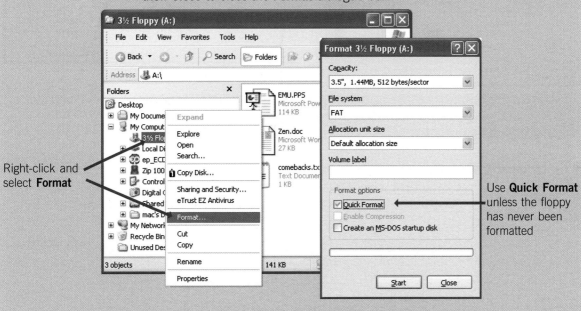

Right-click and select **Format**

Use **Quick Format** unless the floppy has never been formatted

Selecting files and folders

You can select single files by clicking on them, but you can also select a set of files. This is useful when you want to copy files to a floppy disk for backup, or move a set of files into another folder, or delete some that are no longer wanted.

Files can be selected in any view – use whichever works best for you.

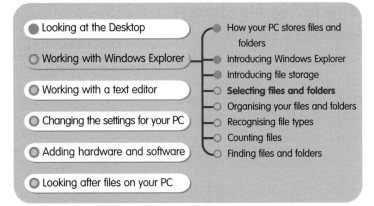

Hold **[Control]** and click to select scattered files

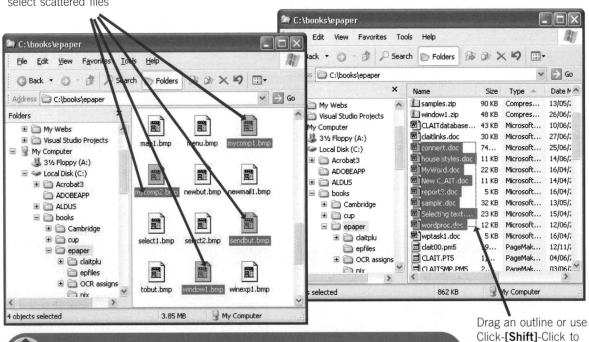

Drag an outline or use Click-**[Shift]**-Click to select a block

> If you want a set of files of the same type or from the same time, use View > Arrange Icons to put them into type or date order before you select.

Skill Builder 2.9

1 Use click and drag to draw a highlight over a set of files to select them.

2 Click on the background to deselect them.

3 Select another block of files using **[Shift]**. Click on the first file, hold **[Shift]** and click on the file at the far end.

4 Deselect the files.

5 Use **[Ctrl]** and click to select some scattered files.

Organising your files and folders

Creating a new folder

A hard drive can hold many thousands of files. The space must be divided into folders if you want to be able to find files quickly. You should create folders to hold your files for each module of this course.

Moving and copying files

- Looking at the Desktop
- Working with Windows Explorer
- Working with a text editor
- Changing the settings for your PC
- Adding hardware and software
- Looking after files on your PC

- How your PC stores files and folders
- Introducing Windows Explorer
- Introducing file storage
- Selecting files and folders
- **Organising your files and folders**
- Recognising file types
- Counting files
- Finding files and folders

You can move and copy files and folders, using the same methods.

❖ If you can see both the source and destination folders, you can use **click and drag** (to move) or **[Ctrl] – click and drag** (to copy).

❖ Otherwise, use **Cut** and **Paste** (to move) or **Copy** and **Paste** (to copy).

Use either method to copy the sample files for this module from the *Resources* folder.

Click and drag will copy, not move, if the destination is on another disk. To move files onto another disk by dragging, hold down the right mouse button while you drag. When you release the button, select Move Here.

| Copy Here |
| Move Here |
| Create Shortcuts Here |
| Cancel |

Skill Builder **2.10**

1 Select *My Documents*. Open the **File** menu, click on **New** then select **Folder**. Call the folder '*ECDL workfiles*'.

2 Find the *Resource Bank* folder for this course. Open it, and open the *Module 2* folder.

3 Select all the documents in *Module 2* and copy them to *ECDL workfiles*.

4 Move *secondtext.txt* from *ECDL workfiles* to your formatted floppy disk.

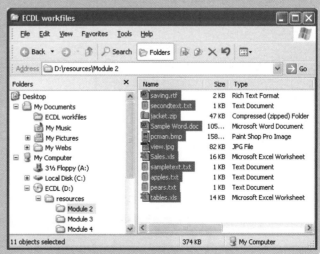

Deleting and the Recycle Bin

When you delete a file or folder, it is not actually removed, but is instead moved to the Recycle Bin. Until you empty the Recycle Bin, any deleted files and folders can be restored. If the folder that they were in has also been deleted, that is recreated first, so files go back into their original place.

Skill Builder **2.11**

1 Delete the file *sampletext.txt* from your *ECDL workfiles* folder.

2 Double-click on its Desktop icon to open the Recycle Bin.

3 Right-click on *sampletext.txt* and select **Restore**.

You can also restore a selected file using **Restore** on the **File** menu

Look at what other files are in the Recycle Bin. If you are sure that you will not want any of them, empty the Bin.

4 Make sure that no files are selected – if they are, click anywhere on the background to deselect them.

5 Open the **File** menu and select **Empty Recycle Bin**.

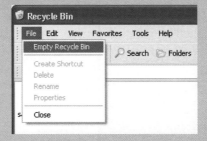

6 You will be asked if you really want to delete them – click **Yes**.

> The Recycle Bin does not cover floppy disks. If you delete a file from a floppy, it cannot be restored.

Recognising file types and counting files

Every file name has an extension which identifies its type, and tells Windows which icon to display and which program to use to open it. The extensions are normally hidden, but can be shown if you like.

- Looking at the Desktop
  - How your PC stores files and folders
- Working with Windows Explorer
  - Introducing Windows Explorer
  - Introducing file storage
- Working with a text editor
  - Selecting files and folders
  - Organising your files and folders
- Changing the settings for your PC
  - **Recognising file types**
  - **Counting files**
- Adding hardware and software
  - Finding files and folders
- Looking after files on your PC

To display file extensions, **View > Folder Options** and open the **View** tab. Look down through the **Advanced settings** options and remove the tick from **Hide file extensions for known file types**.

Skill Builder **2.12**

1 Open the folder *ECDL workfiles*.

2 There are seven types of files. What are they?

3 How many files are there in total?

4 Use **Details** view and arrange the files in **Type** order.

5 Select the text files. How many are there?

6 How many spreadsheet files are there? How much space do they use?

7 How many files start with 's'? What is the quickest way to find out?

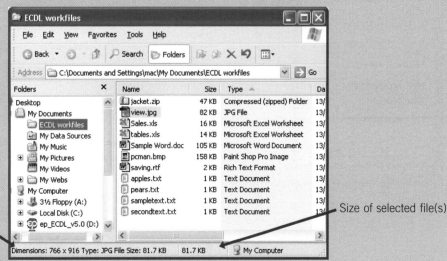

In Windows XP, if a single file is selected, its details are shown in the **Status bar**

Size of selected file(s)

Finding files and folders

Even in a well-organised system, you can forget where you stored a file. The Windows search facility will help you to find lost files. Run this from **Find** on the Start menu in 98 and from **Search** on the Start menu in XP.

If you do not know the full name of the file, you can search for part of the name, or some text in the file, or search by size, date or type. Any or all of these can be specified to narrow down the search.

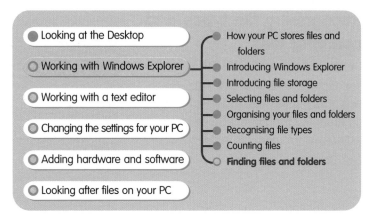

- Looking at the Desktop
- Working with Windows Explorer
- Working with a text editor
- Changing the settings for your PC
- Adding hardware and software
- Looking after files on your PC

- How your PC stores files and folders
- Introducing Windows Explorer
- Introducing file storage
- Selecting files and folders
- Organising your files and folders
- Recognising file types
- Counting files
- **Finding files and folders**

Skill Builder **2.13**

1 Find the program of the Solitaire game, searching for 'sol' – part of its name.

2 Run a new search. Use the **Date and Advanced** options to find files modified in the previous five days, of the type Microsoft Word document (select a different type if you know that Word will not have been used).

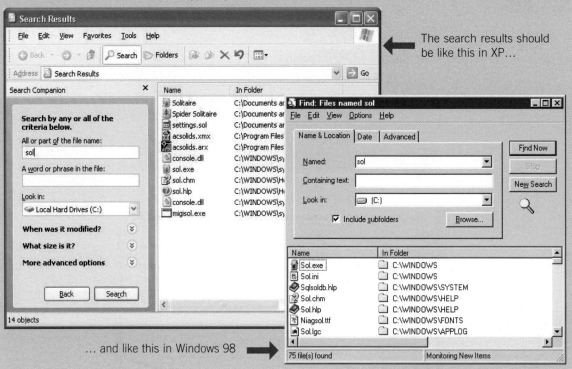

The search results should be like this in XP...

... and like this in Windows 98

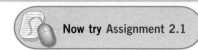
Now try Assignment 2.1

Working with a text editor

Launching WordPad

WordPad is a simple word processor. You can use it to type, edit and format text, for creating letters, reports and similar documents.

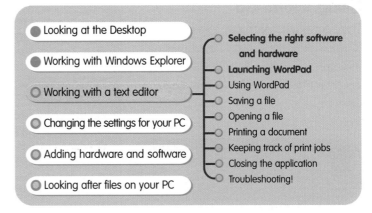

● Looking at the Desktop

● Working with Windows Explorer

○ Working with a text editor

○ Changing the settings for your PC

● Adding hardware and software

○ Looking after files on your PC

○ **Selecting the right software and hardware**
○ **Launching WordPad**
○ Using WordPad
○ Saving a file
○ Opening a file
○ Printing a document
○ Keeping track of print jobs
○ Closing the application
○ Troubleshooting!

Skill Builder 2.14

1   Click **Start**, point to **Programs**, then **Accessories** and click on **WordPad**.

2   Explore the WordPad screen. Pause the mouse over each of the buttons in the toolbars and read the tooltip that will appear.

3   Click on a heading in the **Menu bar** to open up the menu, then point to one of the options – the **Status bar** will display a note about it.

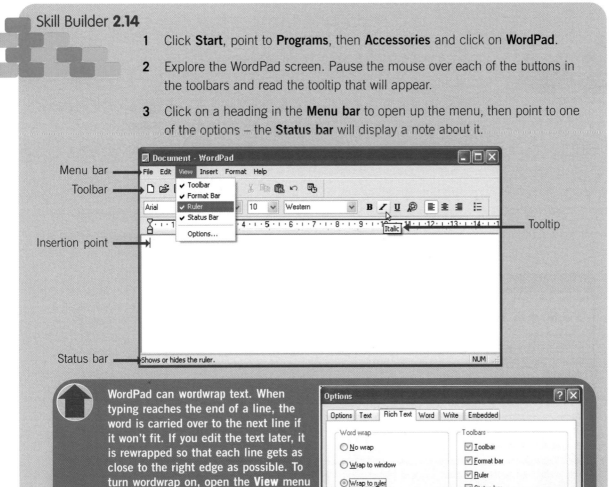

Menu bar
Toolbar
Insertion point
Status bar
Tooltip

WordPad can **wordwrap** text. When typing reaches the end of a line, the word is carried over to the next line if it won't fit. If you edit the text later, it is rewrapped so that each line gets as close to the right edge as possible. To turn wordwrap on, open the **View** menu and select **Options...** On the **Rich Text** tab, select **Wrap to ruler**.

Using WordPad

The best way to learn any application is to use it! And don't worry about making mistakes – learning techniques is more important than accuracy at this stage.

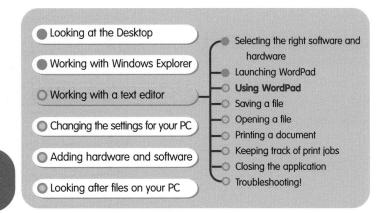

- Looking at the Desktop
- Working with Windows Explorer
- Working with a text editor
- Changing the settings for your PC
- Adding hardware and software
- Looking after files on your PC

- Selecting the right software and hardware
- Launching WordPad
- **Using WordPad**
- Saving a file
- Opening a file
- Printing a document
- Keeping track of print jobs
- Closing the application
- Troubleshooting!

> Remember wordwrap! Only press **[Enter]** at the end of a line if you want to start a new paragraph.

Skill Builder **2.15**

1 Type in these notes about the editing keys.

Editing keys

The Backspace key [<-] erases the character to the left (the one that you have just typed) while the [Delete] key erases the character to the right.

The arrow keys move one character left or right, or one line up or down.

[Home] jumps to the start of the line.

[End] jumps to the end of the line.

Hold [Control] and use the left/right arrows to move one word at a time.

Hold [Control] and use [Home] or [End] to jump to the start or end of the text.

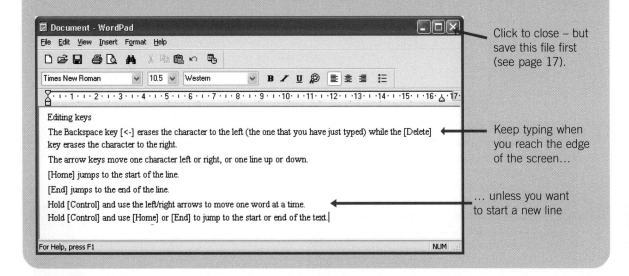

Click to close – but save this file first (see page 17).

Keep typing when you reach the edge of the screen…

… unless you want to start a new line

Saving a file

If you want to use a document again in the future, you must save it. If a document is not saved, it will be lost when you turn off the computer.

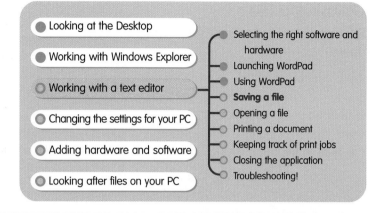

- Looking at the Desktop
- Working with Windows Explorer
- Working with a text editor
- Changing the settings for your PC
- Adding hardware and software
- Looking after files on your PC

- Selecting the right software and hardware
- Launching WordPad
- Using WordPad
- **Saving a file**
- Opening a file
- Printing a document
- Keeping track of print jobs
- Closing the application
- Troubleshooting!

Skill Builder 2.16

1 When you have finished writing your notes, open the **File** menu.

2 Click on **Save As...** The **Save As** dialogue box will open.

3 The **Save in:** box shows the folder in which the file will be saved. If *My Documents* is not the current folder, drop down the list and select it.

4 Double-click on the *ECDL workfiles* folder name or icon to open it.

5 In the **File name:** box, enter the name *editing* to remind you of its subject.

6 Click the **Save** button.

7 Close WordPad.

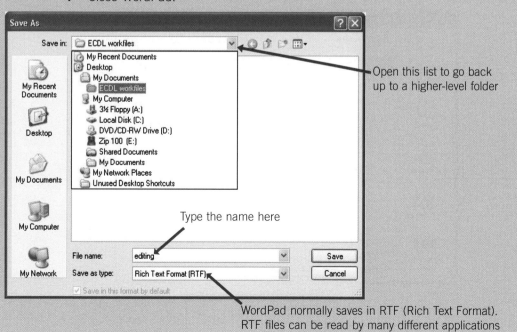

Open this list to go back up to a higher-level folder

Type the name here

WordPad normally saves in RTF (Rich Text Format). RTF files can be read by many different applications

Opening a file

Opening a file is like saving a file – but in reverse.

If you cannot see the file that you want to open, first make sure that the right folder is selected in the **Look in** field, then check that the right type is selected in the **Type of file** field.

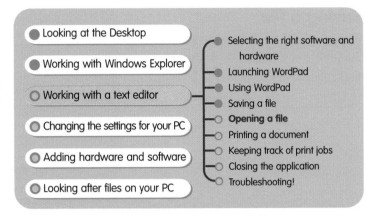

- ● Looking at the Desktop
- ● Working with Windows Explorer
- ○ Working with a text editor
- ◎ Changing the settings for your PC
- ◎ Adding hardware and software
- ◎ Looking after files on your PC

- ● Selecting the right software and hardware
- ● Launching WordPad
- ● Using WordPad
- ● Saving a file
- ○ **Opening a file**
- ○ Printing a document
- ○ Keeping track of print jobs
- ○ Closing the application
- ○ Troubleshooting!

Skill Builder **2.17**

1 Start WordPad. Open the file *saving.rtf* from the *ECDL workfiles* folder.

2 Add the following text at the end of the file.

Save and Save As

Use File > Save when editing an existing file. The new version will replace the old one on the disk. Don't wait until the end before saving. Save early and save often in case Windows crashes or something else goes wrong.

Use File > Save As when you first save a file, or when you want to save a copy with a new name, so that you keep the original version of the file.

Look in the right folder

3 Save the file, but this time with the name *saving2.rtf*.

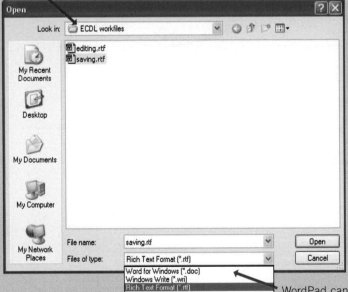

WordPad can open different types of text files and documents created in Word or Write

Printing a document

There are two ways to print a document in WordPad – as there are in most applications.

Click the **Print** button to get one copy on the default printer with the standard settings.

Use the **File > Print** command for a more controlled print.

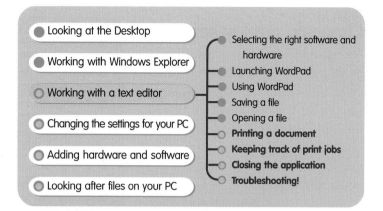

- Looking at the Desktop
- Working with Windows Explorer
- Working with a text editor
- Changing the settings for your PC
- Adding hardware and software
- Looking after files on your PC

- Selecting the right software and hardware
- Launching WordPad
- Using WordPad
- Saving a file
- Opening a file
- **Printing a document**
- **Keeping track of print jobs**
- **Closing the application**
- **Troubleshooting!**

Before you print, check that your printer is turned on and has paper in it. If you are on a network, find out which printer normally handles the output from your PC.

Skill Builder **2.18**

1 In WordPad, open the file *saving2.rtf*.

2 Open the **File** menu and select **Print**. The Print dialogue box will open.

3 If necessary, click on a printer to select it.

4 To print only selected **Pages** type the numbers (e.g. 1,3,5) or the range (1–4).

5 If you want more than one copy, enter the **Number of copies**.

6 Click **Print**.

7 Close WordPad by using **File > Exit** or by clicking the **Close** button.

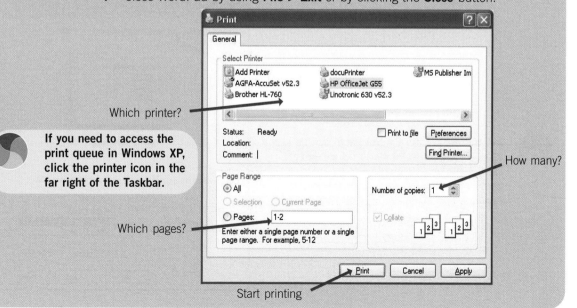

Which printer?

If you need to access the print queue in Windows XP, click the printer icon in the far right of the Taskbar.

How many?

Which pages?

Start printing

Changing the settings for your PC

Changing display settings

The screen of a modern monitor, may be capable of resolutions from 640×480 up to 1600×1200. Very high resolutions can display a lot of information, but the text and icons may be too small to see clearly. Explore the settings on your monitor and find the resolution that works best for you.

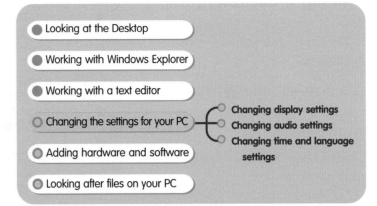

- Looking at the Desktop
- Working with Windows Explorer
- Working with a text editor
- Changing the settings for your PC
  - Changing display settings
  - Changing audio settings
  - Changing time and language settings
- Adding hardware and software
- Looking after files on your PC

Skill Builder 2.19

1   Right-click on the background of the desktop and select **Properties**.

2   Click on the **Settings** tab.

3   Set the **Screen resolution** to its lowest and click **Apply**. How easy is it to see your work and read the screen?

4   Try each higher level of resolution until you find one that gives you the best balance of text size and space on the desktop.

5   Switch to the **Desktop** tab (the **Background** tab in Windows 98/Me) and select a picture or pattern to decorate the desktop.

6   Switch to the **Appearance** tab and change the colour scheme.

Set the background image, pattern or colour

Control the screen saver

In Windows XP, the Control Panel can be in Classic View (as in Windows 98) or Category View, with icons grouped by type. The keyboard language can be changed in the Regional and Language options dialogue box.

Drag to set the resolution

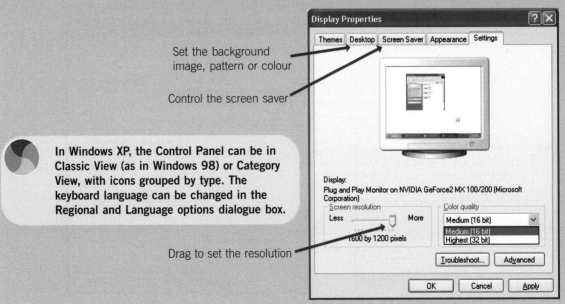

Adding hardware and software

If a computer system is working properly, think carefully before you make any changes to it – things may go wrong and can take time to sort out.

If it is not your computer system, you should not make any changes to the hardware or software without the permission of the owner or network manager.

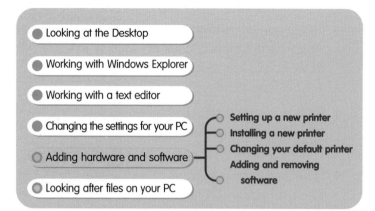

● Looking at the Desktop

● Working with Windows Explorer

● Working with a text editor

● Changing the settings for your PC

○ Adding hardware and software

○ Looking after files on your PC

○ Setting up a new printer
○ Installing a new printer
○ Changing your default printer
○ Adding and removing software

Skill Builder **2.20**

1 Open the *Printers* folder.

2 If there is only one printer present, use **Add printer** to add the **Generic – Text only** printer. (This simplest of printers is useful for testing purposes.)

3 Change the default printer to any other. Then change it back again – it was probably the default for a good reason!

4 If you added the Generic Text only printer, right-click on its icon and select **Delete** to remove it.

5 Close the *Printers* folder.

6 Go to the **Control Panel**, select **Add or Remove Programs** and work through the display to see which programs are installed. Do not remove any unless this is your own computer and you are sure that you will not want to use them again.

Looking after files on your PC

Three main ways to protect your files:

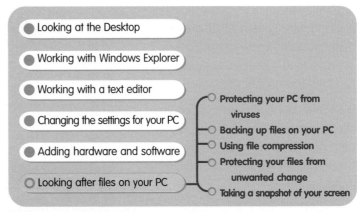

❖ Protect your PC from viruses by installing anti-virus software and by taking care with messages or files that may contain viruses.

❖ Back up files by copying them onto disk or tapes that are then stored away from the PC.

❖ Make them read-only so that others can read but not edit them.

- Looking at the Desktop
- Working with Windows Explorer
- Working with a text editor
- Changing the settings for your PC
- Adding hardware and software
- Looking after files on your PC

○ Protecting your PC from viruses
○ Backing up files on your PC
○ Using file compression
○ Protecting your files from unwanted change
○ Taking a snapshot of your screen

Skill Builder 2.21

1   Run Windows Explorer and go to your *ECDL workfiles* folder.

2   Place your formatted disk (from Skill Builder 2.8) in the A: drive.

3   Copy the file *view.jpg* onto the floppy disk.

4   Open the file *jacket.zip*. Extract its files into the *ECDL workfiles* folder.

5   Create a new compressed file, copying into it all the text files, i.e. those with a .txt, .rtf or .doc extension. Call the new file *sampletext.zip*.

6   Copy *sampletext.zip* onto the floppy disk.

7   Make both files 'Read only' to help protect them.

WinZip compression is built into Windows XP.

To create a new zip file, select the files to be compressed, right-click and select Send To > Compressed Folder.

The 'folder' is a zip file. Its name will be taken from one of the selected files. Rename it if you need to identify it more clearly.

Now try Assignment 2.2

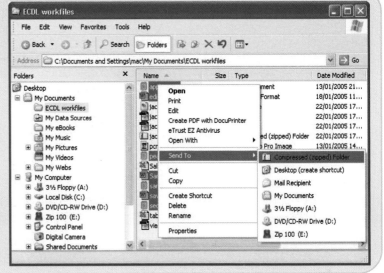

Module 3

WORD PROCESSING

There are two types of programs for producing text:

Text editors, such as WordPad, are used for plain text files, e.g. the source code of programs or web pages. Text editors have few facilities but are small and quick to run.

Word processors, such as Microsoft Word, give you full control over the appearance of text – its size, shape, colour, position – and of its layout on the page. You can add running heads, page numbers and footnotes to every page or to selected pages. You can import images and data from other applications, and can generate contents lists and indexes. Word also has spelling and grammar checkers, and a thesaurus. All these add to the size of the program – Word is nearly 9Mb – so that it takes longer to start, runs slower, and uses far more memory than a text editor.

- ◉ Using the computer and managing files
- ◯ Word processing
- ◯ Spreadsheets
- ◯ Databases
- ◯ Presentations
- ◯ Information and communication

 Throughout this unit you will be asked to open files that are supplied in the Resource Bank. They can be found on the Resource Bank CD or in the folder which your tutor may have set up for use with this course.

Getting started

Menu and toolbar basics

In Word, as in all true Windows applications, all of its features can be reached through the menu system. Most are also available as toolbar buttons, and the ones that you will use most often are on the **Standard** and **Formatting** toolbars. Get to know them.

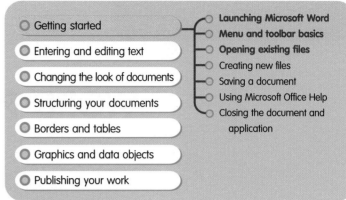

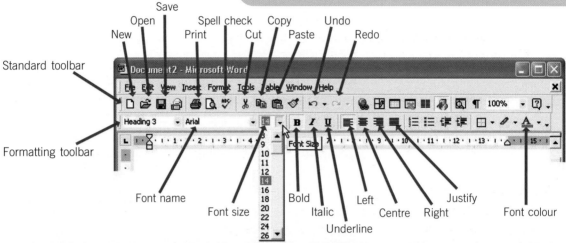

Skill Builder **3.1**

1 Launch Word from the **Start** menu or Desktop.

2 Point to each button in turn on the **Standard** and **Formatting** toolbars and read the screen tip that appears.

3 If a button has an arrow to its right, click the arrow to see the options that drop down from it.

4 Use the **File** menu option or the 📂 toolbar button to open the file *Sample Word.doc* from the *Module 2* folder in the Resource Bank.

Word can open many types of text-based documents. If you are having trouble locating a file in a folder, set the **Files of type** to the appropriate type.

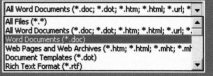

Creating new files

Documents can be started from a blank document, or from templates which have the formatting, layout and perhaps some standard text already set up. We will usually start from blank documents.

Ignore any mistakes. You can correct them once you have learnt about editing.

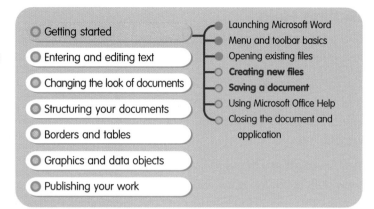

 In Word 2000 **File > New** opens the **New** dialogue box. The **Blank document** option is on the **General** tab.

In Word 2002/2003 **File > New** opens the **New document** task pane. **Blank document** is in the **New** section.

The New Document task pane in Word 2002/2003

Saving a document

Documents must be saved on disk if you want to use them in the future. Click 🖫 to save the file. When saving for the first time, you must select a **Save in** location and give the file a name.

Skill Builder **3.2**

1 Start a new blank document, and type in the title 'Word file formats'.

2 Click 🖫 or use **File > Save As** to start to save the file, giving it the name *WordSave.doc* and selecting your work folder. Do *not* click **Save** yet.

3 Open the list and see the different formats that Word can save a file as. Make a note of any formats that you recognise.

4 Save the file.

5 Type up your notes about the different formats that you know, adding when and why you might use each type.

6 Save the file again.

Getting Help

The simplest way to get Help in Word is to ask the Assistant for it.

You will be prompted to 'Type a question', but all that it really needs is one or two words that describe what you want to know.

'italics' will get you the same Help as 'How do I format the text in italics?'

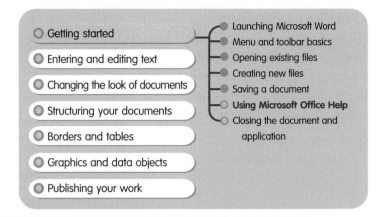

- Getting started
  - Launching Microsoft Word
  - Menu and toolbar basics
  - Opening existing files
  - Creating new files
- Entering and editing text
- Changing the look of documents
  - Saving a document
  - **Using Microsoft Office Help**
- Structuring your documents
  - Closing the document and application
- Borders and tables
- Graphics and data objects
- Publishing your work

 In Word 2000, If the Office Assistant is not visible, click ⑦ to make it appear. Click on the Assistant to wake it up then type your question – or a word or two – into the bubble.

In Word 2002/2003, ask for Help in the 'Type your question here' box at the top right of the Word window.

Skill Builder **3.3**

1   Use Help to find out how to change the colour of text.

2   Use Help to find out how to change the font and size of text.

3   Start a new Word document.

4   Use the Help system to find out more about the Office Assistant. What different Assistants are available? How can you turn the Assistant on and off?

5   Type notes for yourself about the Office Assistant, using the headings: 'Asking for help', 'Choosing an Assistant' and 'Hide and Show'.

6   Format the headings to be Tahoma, 16 point, bold. Format the other text as Georgia, 12 point.

7   Save the file as *WordHelp.doc* in your work folder.

Help window tools

Back to previous Help page

Forward again

Print current page

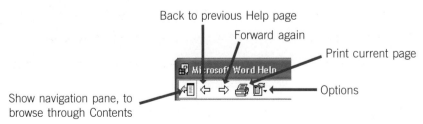

Show navigation pane, to browse through Contents

Options

Closing

You can have any number of Word documents open at once, each one in its own window. The **Close** button at the top right of the title bar will close the document and the window.

When only one document is open, a second **Close** button is present at the end of the menu bar. Clicking this closes the document. Clicking the title bar **Close** button closes the window and exits from Word.

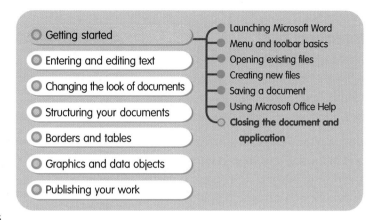

- Getting started
- Entering and editing text
- Changing the look of documents
- Structuring your documents
- Borders and tables
- Graphics and data objects
- Publishing your work

- Launching Microsoft Word
- Menu and toolbar basics
- Opening existing files
- Creating new files
- Saving a document
- Using Microsoft Office Help
- **Closing the document and application**

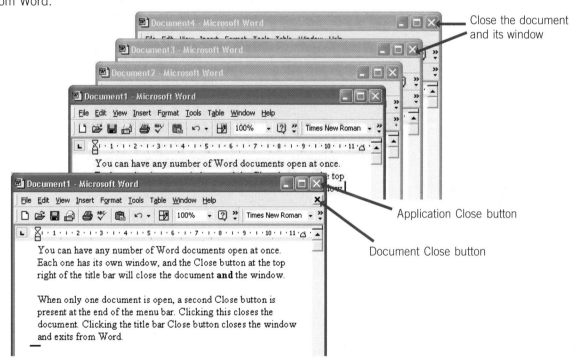

Close the document and its window

Application Close button

Document Close button

You can have any number of Word documents open at once. Each one has its own window, and the Close button at the top right of the title bar will close the document **and** the window.

When only one document is open, a second Close button is present at the end of the menu bar. Clicking this closes the document. Clicking the title bar Close button closes the window and exits from Word.

Skill Builder 3.4

1 Use **File > New** or click ☐ to create a new blank document.

2 Locate the **Close** button to close the new document and its window.

3 There should only be one document open now. Look at the top right of its window. Click ✖ the document **Close** button

4 Click ☒ the application **Close** button to exit from Word.

Entering and editing text

Inserting text

New text is placed at the insertion point – the flashing line. If you want to type in existing text, point and click or use the keys to move the insertion point there.

Do not press **[Enter]** when you reach the end of the line – wordwrap will carry the text over to the next. Only press **[Enter]** at the end of a paragraph or to leave a blank line.

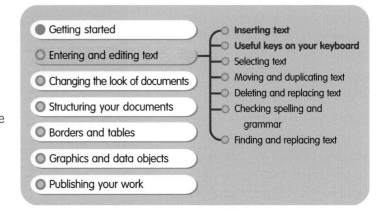

Useful keys

Toggle Insert/Overwrite typing

Delete character to left

start of line

Movement keys

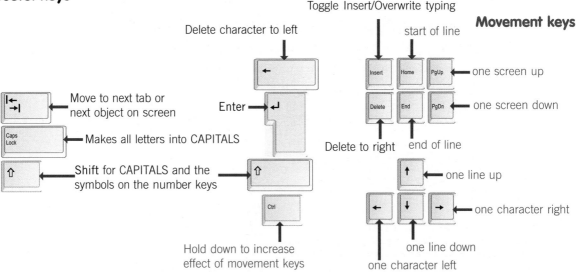

Move to next tab or next object on screen

Enter

one screen up

one screen down

Makes all letters into CAPITALS

Delete to right   end of line

Shift for CAPITALS and the symbols on the number keys

one line up

one character right

Hold down to increase effect of movement keys

one line down

one character left

Skill Builder **3.5**

1   Start a new document.

2   Explore the effects of these keys and type your own notes about them:

   [Home], **[End]**, **[PgUp]**, **[PgDn]**, **[←]**, **[→]**, **[↑]**, **[↓]**, **[Ctrl]**, **[Backspace]** and **[Delete]**.

3   Use the **Insert > Symbol...** routine to find suitable characters for ←, →, ↑, ↓ on the movement keys.

4   Save the document in your work folder with the name *Useful keys.doc*.

Selecting text

Before you can edit or format text, you have to select the text – and before you can do that, you have to have a document open.

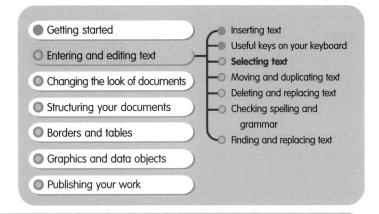

Getting started

Entering and editing text

Changing the look of documents

Structuring your documents

Borders and tables

Graphics and data objects

Publishing your work

Inserting text
Useful keys on your keyboard
Selecting text
Moving and duplicating text
Deleting and replacing text
Checking spelling and grammar
Finding and replacing text

Skill Builder **3.6**

1 Open the *Useful keys.doc* that you created and saved in Skill Builder 3.5.

2 Using click and drag select first a word, a sentence, then a whole paragraph.

3 Repeat the same selections using the **[Shift]** technique, then again using the double-click, **[Ctrl]**-click and triple-click techniques.

4 Save the file as *MyWord.doc*.

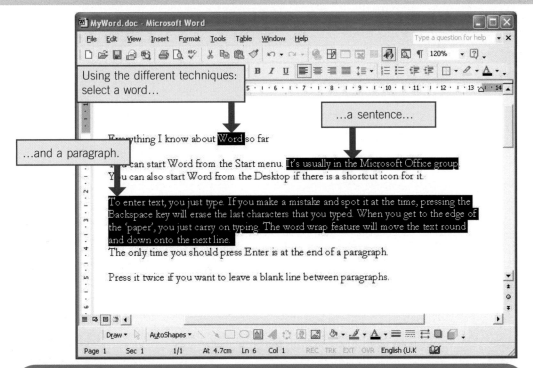

You don't have to select all three blocks of text at once – though it is possible. If you hold down **[Ctrl]** you can select any number of separate blocks using click and drag.

Moving and duplicating text

If you want to use the same text several times, it can be copied. If text is in the wrong place, it can be moved.

Cut, copy and paste

You will find these commands on the **Edit** menu and on the shortcut menus that open when you right-click on something. There are also buttons for them on the Standard toolbar.

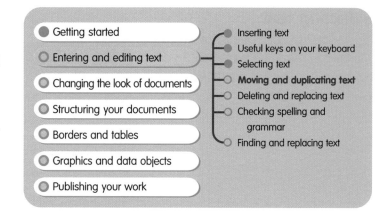

- Getting started
- Entering and editing text
- Changing the look of documents
- Structuring your documents
- Borders and tables
- Graphics and data objects
- Publishing your work

- Inserting text
- Useful keys on your keyboard
- Selecting text
- **Moving and duplicating text**
- Deleting and replacing text
- Checking spelling and grammar
- Finding and replacing text

Copy copies the selected text into a special part of memory called the Clipboard.

Cut deletes the selected data, but places a copy into the Clipboard.

Paste copies the data from the Clipboard into a different place in the same application, or into a different application.

Skill Builder **3.7**

1 Start a new file and type in this list, using copy and paste where appropriate to save retyping words:

Bananas	0.99	per kilo
Cox apples	0.75	per kilo
Melons	1.25	each
Granny Smith apples	1.00	per kilo
Cherries	2.50	per kilo

> Use the **[Tab]** key to line up items in a list

2 Use cut and paste to put the list into alphabetical order.

3 Use drag and drop to put the list into price order.

4 Save the file as *Fruitlist.doc*.

You can copy and paste pictures, files and other objects as well as text, and you can copy data from one Windows application to another.

Deleting and replacing text

To delete characters one at a time, click into the text and press **[Backspace]** to erase to the left of the insertion point or **[Delete]** to erase to the right.

To delete a block of text, select it then press **[Backspace]** or **[Delete]**.

To replace a block, select it then type your new text.

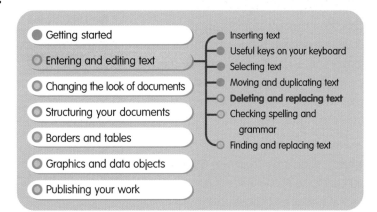

● Getting started	● Inserting text
○ Entering and editing text	● Useful keys on your keyboard
○ Changing the look of documents	● Selecting text
○ Structuring your documents	● Moving and duplicating text
○ Borders and tables	○ **Deleting and replacing text**
○ Graphics and data objects	○ Checking spelling and grammar
○ Publishing your work	○ Finding and replacing text

Skill Builder 3.8

1   Start a new file. Type in the three paragraphs after the heading 'Deleting and replacing' from the top of this page.

2   In the first paragraph, delete the words 'of the insertion point'.

3   In the second paragraph, type 'selected' in front of 'block of text', and delete 'select it then'.

4   In the third paragraph, select 'then' and without deleting it type 'and'.

The text should now read:

To delete characters one at a time, click into the text and press [Backspace] to erase to the left or [Delete] to erase to the right.

To delete a selected block of text, press [Backspace] or [Delete].

To replace a block, select it and type your new text.

5   Save the file as *deleting.doc*.

Undo and Redo

In Word, as in all the Office applications, you can undo a whole series of actions. This protects you from your mistakes, and also sets you free to experiment. You can do major editing and if at the end you preferred the text as it was, you can undo all your changes.

Click the **Undo** button  or select from the list to undo your last action(s).

Use the **Redo** button if you undo too much, to put the changes back again. Use it for the last action, or a whole sequence, as with Undo.

Click to undo the last action.

Drop down the list to undo all the actions back to a selected one.

 You cannot undo (or redo) one action from part-way down the list – all those above are also undone (or redone).

Spell checking

The spell checker's dictionary does not cover everything. Names, technical terms and unusual words may be thrown up as 'errors'. These can be added to your own dictionary, so that they are accepted in future.

Words used in the wrong way, e.g. 'there' when it should be 'their' are not picked up by the spell checker – but might be by the grammar checker.

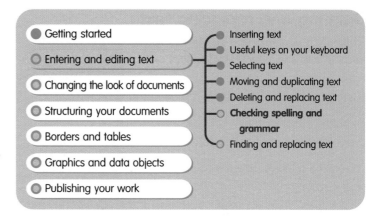

Spelling options

Word has a 'check-as-you-type' option. If you prefer, you can run the spell check and grammar after you have finished.

Check your checking options

1 Open the **Tools** menu and select **Options**.

2 Click on the **Spelling and Grammar** label to bring that tab to the front.

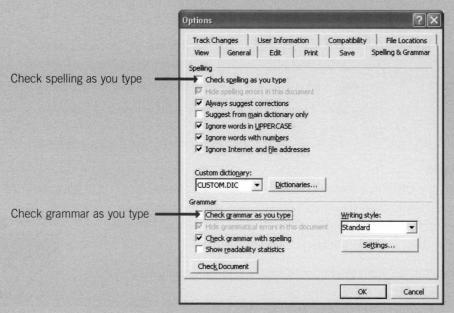

3 Click on the checkbox or on the text beside it to turn the **Check spelling as you type** and **Check grammar as you type** options on ☑ or off ☐.

4 Click **OK** to close the dialogue box and save your settings.

Running a spelling and grammar check

You can check your work at the end of your editing, or at any point while you are working.

Skill Builder 3.9

1. Open oone of your files, e.g. *deleting.doc*.

2. Click the 🗹 **Spelling and Grammar** button on the **Standard** toolbar.

3. When a word is not in the dictionary this dialogue box will appear.

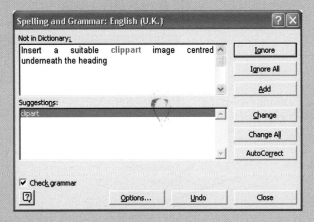

You can:

- Select a **Suggestion** and click **Change**.

- Click **Ignore** if it is a valid word, but you do not want to add it to the dictionary.

- Click **Ignore All** so that any later occurrences of the word are also ignored.

- Click **Add** to put it in a custom dictionary.

- Click into the top pane, edit the word then click **Change**.

> Word 2000 has four Writing style options – *Casual*, *Standard*, *Formal* and *Technical*. You can also set different aspects of the style through the Settings... button.
>
> Word 2002/3 gives you only two Writing style choices – *Grammar only* and *Grammar & Style*, but you can still specify the Style through the Settings... button.
>
> To reach the Settings in either Word, open the Tools menu and select Options, then switch to the Spelling & Grammar tab.

Find and replace

The **Find** facility will locate a given word or phrase in a document. Just enter the word to find, and click **Find Next**.

Replace is an extension of **Find** – the main difference is that you specify the text to insert in place of the found text. It is typically used for updating reports or work schedules.

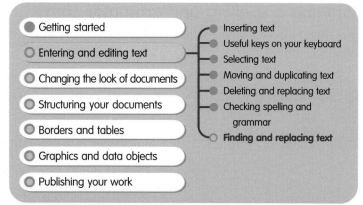

These three options can be useful

Match case – e.g. if looking for 'Smith', ignore 'smith' or 'SMITH'

Find whole words only – e.g. if looking for 'now', ignore 'snow' or 'known'

Sounds like – use for tricky spelling. The word is found if your guess is close enuff…

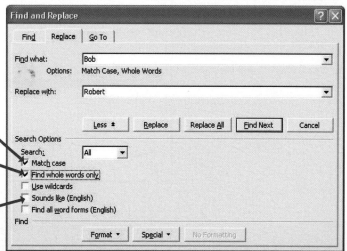

Skill Builder 3.10

1 Type in this text – it's part of a letter to a friend.

I ran into Bob Brown the other day. He was looking well. I asked him what he was doing. He said, "Oh, you know. Ducking and diving, bobbing and weaving. How about you?"

I said, "Can't complain. I'm making a bob or two."

And that was the end of the conversation. He never has been much of a talker, old Bob.

2 Save the file as *bobone.doc*.

3 You have just remembered. You are the only person to call him Bob. Everyone else calls him Robert. Change the name using the **Replace** facility. Will any of the options be useful?

 Now try Assignment 3.1

Changing the look of documents

Formatting text

You can change the font, size, style or colour of any amount of text, from a single character to the whole document. You can format text using the buttons on the Formatting toolbar or the options in the Font dialogue box.

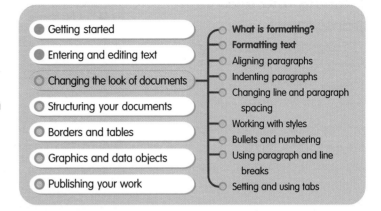

- ● Getting started
- ● Entering and editing text
- ○ Changing the look of documents
- ○ Structuring your documents
- ● Borders and tables
- ● Graphics and data objects
- ● Publishing your work

- ○ What is formatting?
- ○ **Formatting text**
- ○ Aligning paragraphs
- ○ Indenting paragraphs
- ○ Changing line and paragraph spacing
- ○ Working with styles
- ○ Bullets and numbering
- ○ Using paragraph and line breaks
- ○ Setting and using tabs

Skill Builder **3.11**

1. If necessary, start Word. Open your file *MyWord.doc*.

2. Select the first line, and apply the Heading 1 style to it.

3. Select the rest of the text and change its size to 12 point.

4. Make bold each occurrence of 'Word' or 'Microsoft'.

5. If there is the name of a key, e.g. **Enter**, select it and change its font to Arial.

6. Add some new notes under the heading '**Formatting**'. Apply the Heading 2 style to this, and use suitable formatting options to add emphasis to your notes.

7. Save the file with the new name, *MyWord2.doc* and close it.

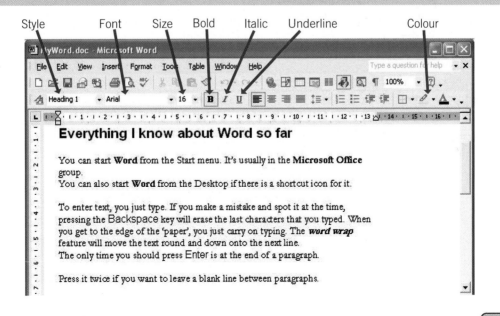

Style   Font   Size   Bold   Italic   Underline   Colour

Aligning and indenting paragraphs

The **alignment** settings control how the text aligns with the left and right margins. You can set the alignment easily using the toolbar buttons.

Indents can be set on the ruler – drag the markers to set the indents. You can also use the toolbar buttons to increase or decrease the left indent.

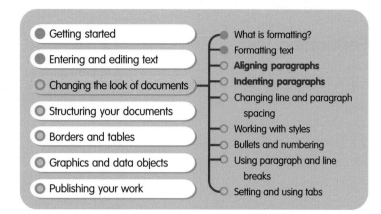

- ● Getting started
- ● Entering and editing text
- ○ Changing the look of documents
- ● Structuring your documents
- ● Borders and tables
- ● Graphics and data objects
- ● Publishing your work

- ● What is formatting?
- ● Formatting text
- ○ **Aligning paragraphs**
- ○ **Indenting paragraphs**
- ○ Changing line and paragraph spacing
- ○ Working with styles
- ○ Bullets and numbering
- ○ Using paragraph and line breaks
- ○ Setting and using tabs

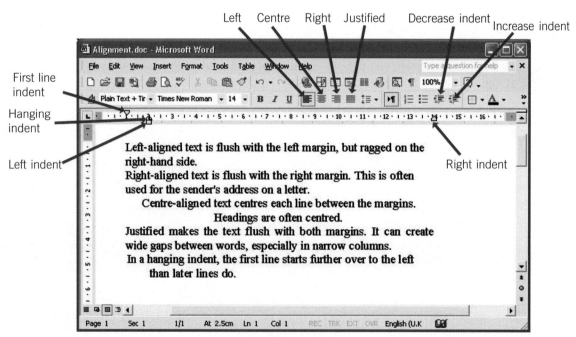

Left · Centre · Right · Justified · Decrease indent · Increase indent

First line indent · Hanging indent · Left indent · Right indent

Left-aligned text is flush with the left margin, but ragged on the right-hand side.
Right-aligned text is flush with the right margin. This is often used for the sender's address on a letter.
Centre-aligned text centres each line between the margins.
Headings are often centred.
Justified makes the text flush with both margins. It can create wide gaps between words, especially in narrow columns.
In a hanging indent, the first line starts further over to the left than later lines do.

Skill Builder 3.12

1 Start a new file and type the notes shown in the screenshot above.

2 Select all the text and increase the font size to 14 point. Drag the left indent marker to 1 cm, and the right indent marker to 14 cm.

3 Set the alignments of the paragraphs to match their topics.

4 Select the last paragraph. Drag the hanging indent marker in to 2 cm. If the first line indent marker moves with it, drag that back out again to 1 cm.

5 Save the file as *Alignment.doc*.

Line and paragraph spacing

Line spacing refers to the space between lines in a paragraph. Common options are single, double and 1.5.

Paragraph spacing refers to the amount of space before or after a paragraph. It is usually measured in points (pt). A 12 point space is about the same as a normal blank line.

Line and paragraph spacing can be set through the **Paragraph** dialogue box.

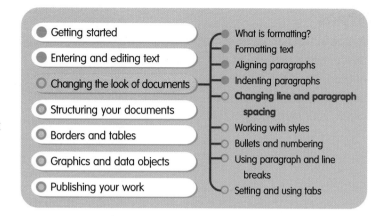

- Getting started
- Entering and editing text
- Changing the look of documents
- Structuring your documents
- Borders and tables
- Graphics and data objects
- Publishing your work

- What is formatting?
- Formatting text
- Aligning paragraphs
- Indenting paragraphs
- **Changing line and paragraph spacing**
- Working with styles
- Bullets and numbering
- Using paragraph and line breaks
- Setting and using tabs

Word 2002/2003 has a **Line spacing** toolbar button 📏⏷ , with a drop-down list that you can use to set single, 1.5, double and triple spacing.

Skill Builder 3.13

1 Open your file *Alignment.doc*.

2 Select all the text and set the paragraph spacing to 6 point after.

3 Set the centre alignment paragraph to 1.5 lines spacing.

4 Save and close the file.

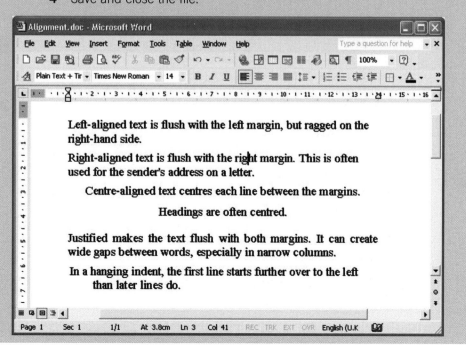

Styles

A style is a combination of font, size, colour, alignment, indent and spacing options. Word has a large set of pre-defined styles. You can modify these, or create your own styles.

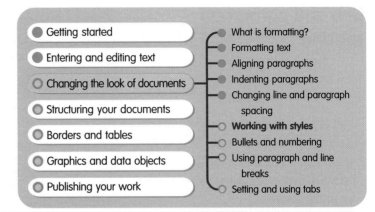

- Getting started
- Entering and editing text
- Changing the look of documents
- Structuring your documents
- Borders and tables
- Graphics and data objects
- Publishing your work

- What is formatting?
- Formatting text
- Aligning paragraphs
- Indenting paragraphs
- Changing line and paragraph spacing
- **Working with styles**
- Bullets and numbering
- Using paragraph and line breaks
- Setting and using tabs

Skill Builder **3.14**

1 Open the supplied file *Styles.doc.* in the Resource Bank *Module 3* folder.

2 Using the **Styles** drop-down list, set 'Styles' to Heading 1; 'Paragraph styles' and 'Character styles' to Heading 2; and 'User-defined styles' to Heading 3.

3 Modify the Heading 3 style. Make it 12 point, and coloured green.

4 Create a new character style, called *Emphatic*, based on *Normal.* Turn bold and italic on, and set the colour to red. Apply it to 'style' in the second line.

5 Create a new character style, called *Computer*, based on no style. Set the font to Sans Serif or Arial, size 10, with bold on, and coloured navy. Apply it to 'Font' and 'Paragraph' in the 'Character styles' paragraph.

6 Save the document in your work folder, and close it.

The document should look like this after applying the styles

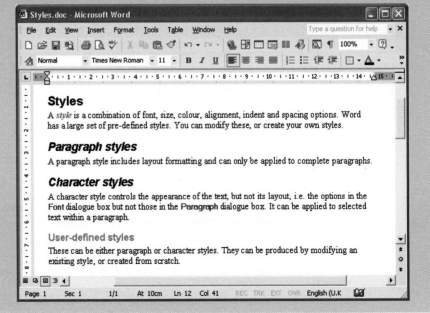

Bullets and numbering

Bullets or numbers can be applied to lists using the toolbar buttons. Their appearance can be modified through the Bullets and Numbering dialogue box.

If you start a list by typing **1** then pressing **[Tab]** before the text, Word will add numbers to all later lines automatically.

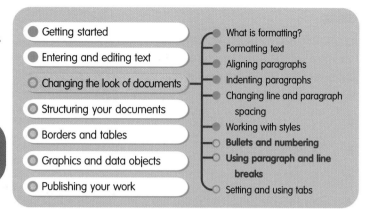

- Getting started
- Entering and editing text
- Changing the look of documents
- Structuring your documents
- Borders and tables
- Graphics and data objects
- Publishing your work

- What is formatting?
- Formatting text
- Aligning paragraphs
- Indenting paragraphs
- Changing line and paragraph spacing
- Working with styles
- **Bullets and numbering**
- **Using paragraph and line breaks**
- Setting and using tabs

Skill Builder **3.15**

1 Open the supplied file *bullets.doc* in the Resource Bank *Module 3* folder.

2 Apply Heading 1 to the first line, then add numbering to the rest of the lines.

3 Select the lines numbered 4 and 5. Remove the numbering and add bullets.

4 Select the bulleted lines, right-click and select **Bullets and Numbering...** to open the dialogue box. Change the bullet to a picture.

The document should look like this after adding the numbers and bullets

These had been lines 4 and 5 when numbering was first applied

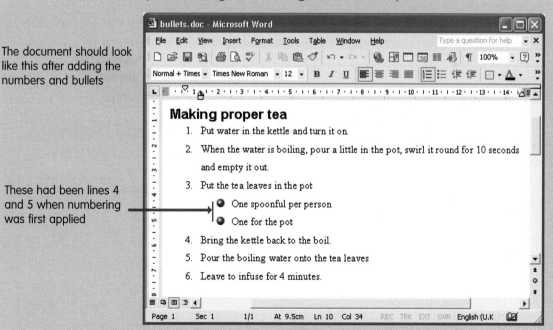

To set picture bullets in Word 2002/3, first click the **Customize...** button, then click the **Picture...** button in the **Customize Bulleted List** dialogue box.

Tabs

By default, there are left tab every ½"
(12 mm). These are easily replaced –
just select the style from the tab well and
click on the ruler.

| ⌐ | Text aligns with the tab on the left |

⌐ Text aligns with the tab on the left

⊥ Text centres on the tab

⌐ Text aligns with the tab on the right

⊥ Decimal point aligns with the tab

| Draws a vertical bar at the tab

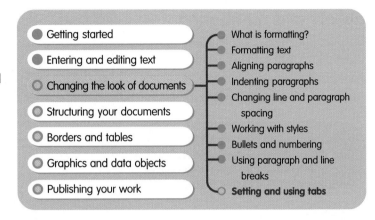

- Getting started
- Entering and editing text
- Changing the look of documents
- Structuring your documents
- Borders and tables
- Graphics and data objects
- Publishing your work

- What is formatting?
- Formatting text
- Aligning paragraphs
- Indenting paragraphs
- Changing line and paragraph spacing
- Working with styles
- Bullets and numbering
- Using paragraph and line breaks
- **Setting and using tabs**

Skill Builder **3.16**

1 Open the supplied file *tabs.doc.* in the Resource Bank *Module 3* folder.

2 Select all the text. Place left tabs at approximately 1 cm and 2.5 cm, and a right tab at 10 cm.

3 With the text still selected, open the **Format** menu and select **Tabs...**

4 Select the 10 cm tab. In the **Leader** section, select option **2......** and click **Set** to add dots to the tab, then **OK** to close the dialogue box.

5 Save the file in your work folder, and close it.

Tab well

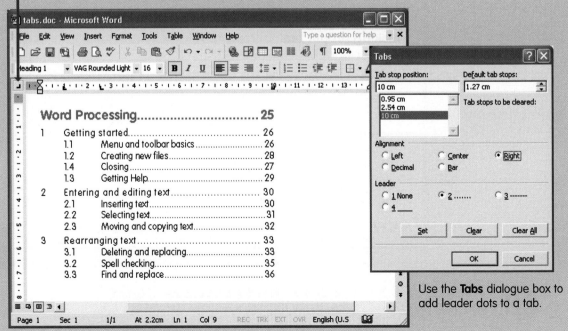

Use the **Tabs** dialogue box to add leader dots to a tab.

Structuring your documents

Headers and footers

Headers and footers appear at the top and bottom of every page. They can display the page number, date and time, filename, author and similar file details, or any typed text.

The page number, date, and other details can be inserted from the **Header and Footer** toolbar button or the **Autotext** list.

The header and footer have tabs in place so that items can go on the left, centre or right.

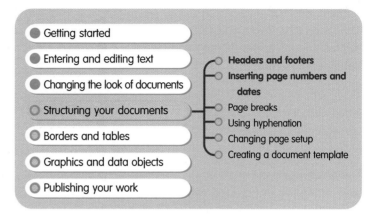

- Getting started
- Entering and editing text
- Changing the look of documents
- Structuring your documents
- Borders and tables
- Graphics and data objects
- Publishing your work

- Headers and footers
- Inserting page numbers and dates
- Page breaks
- Using hyphenation
- Changing page setup
- Creating a document template

Header/footer tools

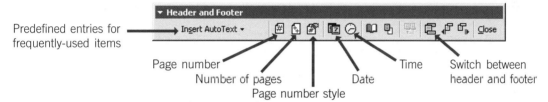

Predefined entries for frequently-used items

Page number
Number of pages
Page number style
Date
Time
Switch between header and footer

Skill Builder 3.17

1 Start a new document.

2 Go into **Header and Footer** view.

3 Type your name in the left of the header, then format it in Arial, 9 point.

4 Press **[Tab]** to move to the centre of the header. Use the toolbar button to insert the date.

5 Switch to the footer. Use the toolbar button to insert the page number, and format it in Times New Roman, 10 point, bold.

6 Click **Close** to close the **Header and Footer** toolbar and return to the text.

7 Double-click to go back into the header and format the date in Arial, 8 point, then use the double-click method to return to the text.

Page Setup

The paper size, layout and margin options and are all set through the **Page Setup** dialogue box.

In the UK, the most commonly used paper size is A4. The orientation is normally portrait, i.e. taller than it is wide.

The margins are the areas around the edge of the page where text cannot be typed. They are normally the same for the whole document.

Where pages are to be printed on both sides, and then bound, the left and right-hand pages may be different. If so, turn on **Mirror margins**. Left and Right margins are then replaced by Inside and Outside margins.

The *gutter* is an extra margin to allow for stapling or binding, and can be either on the inside or top of the page.

- Getting started
- Entering and editing text
- Changing the look of documents
- Structuring your documents
  - Headers and footers
  - Inserting page numbers and dates
  - **Page breaks**
  - **Using hyphenation**
  - **Changing page setup**
  - Creating a document template
- Borders and tables
- Graphics and data objects
- Publishing your work

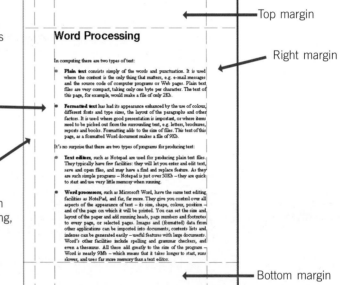

Top margin

Right margin

Left margin

Gutter

Bottom margin

Skill Builder **3.18**

1. Open *Alignment.doc* (or any of your work files).

2. Set these margins:

Top	2.5 cm (1")	Bottom	3 cm (1.2")
Left	2 cm (0.8")	Right	2 cm (0.8")
Gutter (left)	1 cm (0.4")		

3. Try to set the Bottom margin to 1 cm (0.4"). What happens? Word insists that you leave room for a 'footer' – a space at the bottom where the page number, file name and similar things can be written.

Creating a document template

All documents start from some kind of template which sets up the basic design. Even the 'blank document' is a template, though this simply sets the page size and defines the styles. Other templates may have more elaborate design features and suggestions for content and layout of the items to include in the new document.

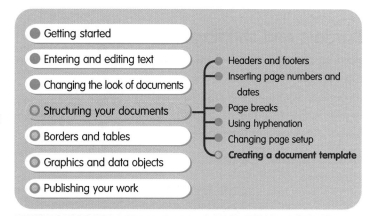

- Getting started
- Entering and editing text
- Changing the look of documents
- Structuring your documents
- Borders and tables
- Graphics and data objects
- Publishing your work

  - Headers and footers
  - Inserting page numbers and dates
  - Page breaks
  - Using hyphenation
  - Changing page setup
  - **Creating a document template**

Skill Builder **3.19**

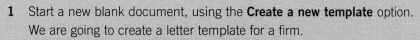

1 Start a new blank document, using the **Create a new template** option. We are going to create a letter template for a firm.

2 Modify the Normal style to make it the font Tahoma (or Arial), 11 point, and the paragraph set to Justified, with 6 point space above.

3 At the top of the page, type the name, address and telephone number on three lines: 'International Exports', 'International House, 21 Bridge Road, Westown', 'Tel: 0044 0555 1234'.

4 Format the name in a script font, e.g. Monotype Corsiva, 30 point and colour it blue. Use Normal style for the address and telephone number. Centre align the whole address block.

5 Insert the date on the left below the address. Turn on the **Update Automatically** option. (Why?)

6 Save the file as a template, with the name *International.dot*. Close the file.

Your template should look like this – the grey background to the date shows that it is a field (a special form of data) and will be updated. This shading is not printed.

Now try Assignment 3.2

Borders and tables

Borders and shading

You can add emphasis to a heading or a block of text by adding borders to one or more of its edges, or shading the area behind it. Borders and shading can be set from the **Tables and Borders** toolbar.

We can use them to enhance our letterhead.

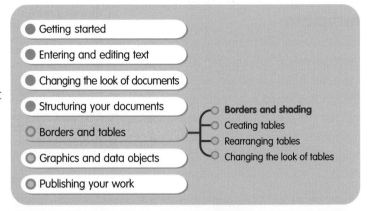

- Getting started
- Entering and editing text
- Changing the look of documents
- Structuring your documents
- Borders and tables
  - **Borders and shading**
  - Creating tables
  - Rearranging tables
  - Changing the look of tables
- Graphics and data objects
- Publishing your work

Skill Builder **3.20**

1 Start a new file from a template, using your *International.dot*.

2 Click ▦ to display the **Tables and Borders** toolbar.

3 Click into the name line and add a pale shading to it.

4 Click into the telephone number line and add a bottom border, so that a line is drawn across the page.

5 Save the file, as a template, with the name *International Letter.dot*. Close the file.

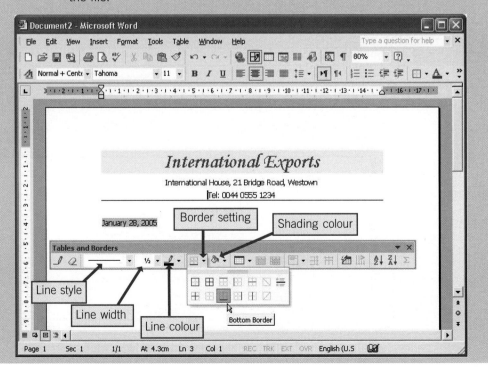

Creating and formatting tables

If you need to lay out text or data in columns and rows, you can do it with tabs, but it's simpler to insert a table. A table can be of any size, and rows and columns can be inserted or deleted later if you need to change the size.

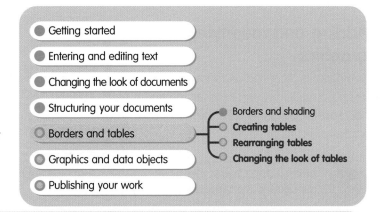

- Getting started
- Entering and editing text
- Changing the look of documents
- Structuring your documents
- Borders and tables
  - Borders and shading
  - **Creating tables**
  - **Rearranging tables**
  - **Changing the look of tables**
- Graphics and data objects
- Publishing your work

Skill Builder 3.21

1 Start a new file. We are going to produce a simple leaflet for a pizza firm.

2 At the top of the page type 'The Leading Tower of Pizza'. Format it with a large, loud font and centre the text.

3 Insert a table of 4 rows and 5 columns. Enter this text:

	Meat feast	Four cheese	Anchovy and olives	Vegetarian delight
Small	4.99	4.49	4.69	3.99
Medium	6.99	6.49	6.75	5.49
Family	9.99	9.49	9.99	8.25

4 Embolden all the headings, and centre the prices and column headings.

5 Give the table a thick, bright border.

6 Give the columns different fill colours.

7 Insert a new line below '**Medium**', with the heading '**Large**'. The prices are all £1.50 more than the medium pizzas in the same columns.

8 Save the file as *pizzas.doc*.

The table formatting tools

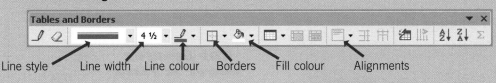

Line style   Line width   Line colour   Borders   Fill colour   Alignments

Your finished table should look something like this – with your own choice of colours

	Meat feast	Four cheese	Anchovy and olives	Vegetarian delight
Small	4.99	4.49	4.69	3.99
Medium	6.99	6.49	6.75	5.49
Large	7.49	7.99	8.25	6.99
Family	9.99	9.49	9.99	8.25

Graphics and data objects

Adding and modifying graphics

Photographs, scanned and drawn images and clip art can be inserted into documents. The same tools can be used with all types of graphics.

 In Word 2002/2003, clip art is managed in the task pane.

- Getting started
- Entering and editing text
- Changing the look of documents
  - Adding graphics
  - Modifying graphics
  - Copying data from other applications
  - Importing blank worksheets and charts
- Structuring your documents
- Borders and tables
- Graphics and data objects
- Publishing your work
  - Changing the look of an imported chart

Clip art in Word 2002/2003

1 Place the insertion point where you want the clip art.

2 Use **Insert > Picture > Clip Art**.

3 In the **Insert Clip Art** task pane, type one or more words to describe what you are looking for and click **Search**.

4 Scroll through the matching images.

5 To insert an image, double-click on it.

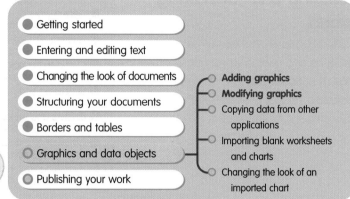

What do you want?

There may be dozens of matching images

Skill Builder **3.22**

1 Open *pizzas.doc*.

2 Click to place the insertion point below the left of the heading.

3 Insert the image *pizza logo.bmp* from the Resource Bank *Module 3* folder.

4 Reduce the image to about half its size.

5 Set its text wrap to square and drag it to the right of the heading.

6 Save the file.

Your document should look something like this

Key tools on the Picture toolbar

Brightness +/–   Rotate   Border   Format picture

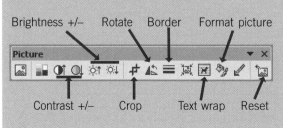

Contrast +/–   Crop   Text wrap   Reset

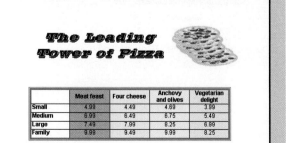

Copying and importing data

Data can be copied in from many Windows applications. You can also import or create objects from other Office applications in your Word documents.

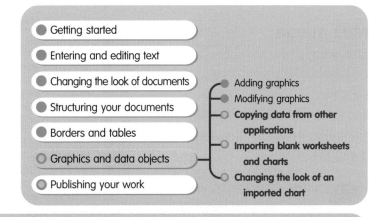

- Getting started
- Entering and editing text
- Changing the look of documents
  - Adding graphics
  - Modifying graphics
  - **Copying data from other applications**
  - **Importing blank worksheets and charts**
  - **Changing the look of an imported chart**
- Structuring your documents
- Borders and tables
- Graphics and data objects
- Publishing your work

Skill Builder **3.23**

1 Run Excel and open *pizzas.xls* from the Resource Bank *Module 3* folder.

2 Copy the chart to the Clipboard.

3 Open *pizzas.doc.*

4 Move the insertion point below the table and type the heading 'Our most popular pizzas'. Format this in Arial 16 point, bold, centre aligned.

5 Paste in the chart. Move it to beneath the new heading.

6 Change the colour of each slice so that it matches the colour in the table.

7 Save the file.

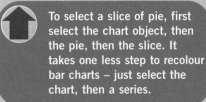

To select a slice of pie, first select the chart object, then the pie, then the slice. It takes one less step to recolour bar charts – just select the chart, then a series.

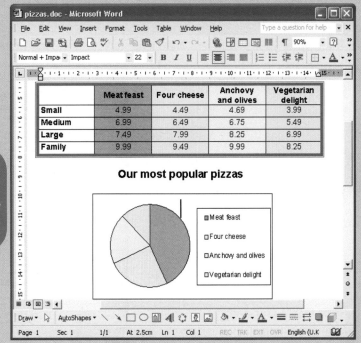

Publishing your work

Mail merge

Mail merge allows you to produce personalised letters and labels quickly and easily.

You can use an existing main document and merge a data file or create them during the merge.

 In Word 2002/2003, mail merge is handled in the task pane.

- Getting started
- Entering and editing text
- Changing the look of documents
- Structuring your documents
- Borders and tables
- Graphics and data objects
- Publishing your work

- **Introduction to mail merge**
- **Using mail merge**
- **Creating and printing mailing labels**
- Previewing documents
- Printing documents
- Publishing documents for the Web
- Changing your personal settings

Mail merge in Word 2002/2003

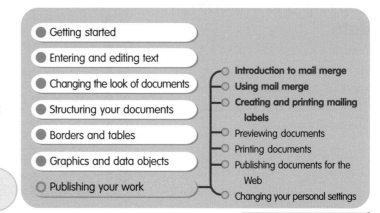

1   When the document is ready, save it, then open the **Tools** menu, point to **Letters and Mailings** and select **Mail Merge Wizard...**

2   Select the **document type** and click **Next**.

3   Select the **starting document** – either the current document or one from file – then click **Next**.

4   If the recipient list is in an existing data file, click **Browse** to find it. A wizard will run to ensure that the data is imported properly.

    If you choose **Type a new list**, the **New Address List** dialogue box will open and the address information should be entered, and saved.

5   At the **Write your letter** step, if the letter has not yet been written, or it needs editing, the text can be typed now.

6   Place the insertion point where you want the first field to be written.

7   The wizard has a ready-made **Address block**, and **Greeting line** which will bring in the relevant fields – if standard field names are used. If not, use the **More items...** link to select individual fields.

8   Click **Next** to preview your letters. Check through enough of them to see how the merge will work. If the text or fields need to be edited, do that now.

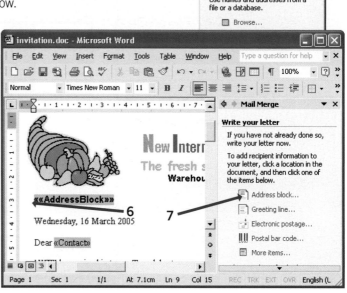

8 Click **Next** to complete the merge.

9 If no further editing is required, click **Print**, select the records to print and click **OK**.

10 If you want to personalise the mailing, click **Edit individual letters** and edit selected merged letters as required before printing.

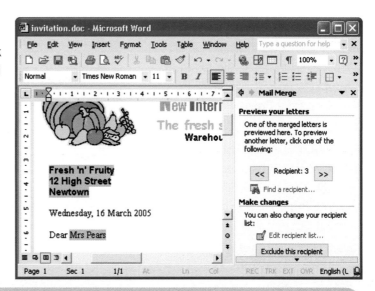

Skill Builder **3.24**

1 Open *invitation.doc* in the Resource Bank *Module 3* folder.

2 Start a mail merge, using this as the main document.

3 For the data source, use the file *clients.csv* in the *Module 3* folder.

4 Insert the fields *Company, Address1* and *Address2* above the date. (These wil be selected for the Address block in Word 2002/2003.)

5 Insert the field *Contact* after 'Dear'.

6 Merge the document and data source.

7 Save the merged document as *merged invitations.doc*.

Now for some mailing labels.

8 Start a new blank document.

9 Set the label type to Avery 3261L, or any size that will give you two columns.

10 Copy the name and address details from the letter, and paste them at the top of the label. Reformat the text to Arial, 8 point, black, left aligned.

11 Use the same data source, and add these fields to the label: *Contact, Company, Address1* and *Address1*.

12 Save the merged document as *merged labels.doc*.

The labels should look like this

Previewing and printing

Word is a WYSIWYG (What You See Is What You Get) system, but the **Print Layout** view doesn't always tell the whole story. Use **Print Preview** to check before you print.

To print one copy of a document on the default printer with the default settings, click 🖨, or other use **File > Print** to open the **Print** dialogue box.

- ● Getting started
- ● Entering and editing text
- ● Changing the look of documents
- ● Structuring your documents
- ● Borders and tables
- ● Graphics and data objects
- ○ Publishing your work

  - ● Introduction to mail merge
  - ● Using mail merge
  - ● Creating and printing mailing labels
  - ○ **Previewing documents**
  - ○ **Printing documents**
  - ○ Publishing documents for the Web
  - ○ Changing your personal settings

Skill Builder **3.25**

1   Open your file *merged labels.doc*.

2   Preview the document.

3   Print one copy of the document on the default printer.

4   Open your file *merged invitations.doc*.

5   Preview the document.

6   Select a colour printer, if one can be accessed from your PC.

7   Print one copy of pages 1 and 3.

To print specific pages, type the page numbers, or ranges of pages, separated by commas, like this: 1,3,5-7,10

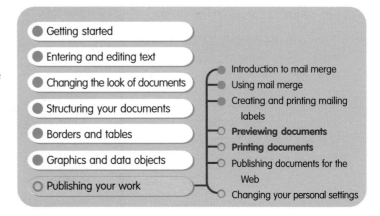

Creating Web pages

Word has a Wizard that makes it easy to create a set of linked web pages. You can also save any Word document as a web page. These can be linked into your web site by the wizard.

In this exercise you will create a skeleton web site for a firm.

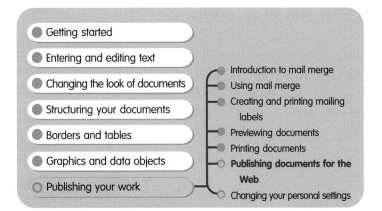

- Getting started
- Entering and editing text
- Changing the look of documents
- Structuring your documents
- Borders and tables
- Graphics and data objects
- Publishing your work

  - Introduction to mail merge
  - Using mail merge
  - Creating and printing mailing labels
  - Previewing documents
  - Printing documents
  - **Publishing documents for the Web**
  - Changing your personal settings

Skill Builder 3.26

1 Start a new document from the Web Page Wizard.

2 Give the site the title 'IntImports' and save it in your work folder.

3 Use a vertical or horizontal frame layout.

4 At the **Add Pages** stage, add two blank pages but remove the Personal Web Page.

5 Rename the pages 'Home', 'Contact Us', 'Product Range' and 'Special Offers'.

6 Add the *Industrial* visual theme.

7 Click **Finish** to end the wizard.

8 On the home page, type 'Welcome to International Imports' and format it with a large distinctive type.

To change the size of the frames, click on the boundary between them and drag the dark line

Changing your settings

You should check that your name is there in the User Information, and that the right file locations are set as the defaults. There are other options that are also worth checking – but if you don't know how an option affects your documents, leave it at the default.

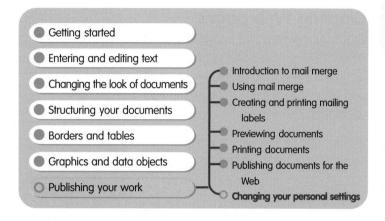

- Getting started
- Entering and editing text
- Changing the look of documents
- Structuring your documents
- Borders and tables
- Graphics and data objects
- Publishing your work
  - Introduction to mail merge
  - Using mail merge
  - Creating and printing mailing labels
  - Previewing documents
  - Printing documents
  - Publishing documents for the Web
  - **Changing your personal settings**

Skill Builder **3.27**

1   Open the **Options** dialogue box.

2   On the **User Information** tab, type your name and initials.

3   On the **View**, **General** and **Edit** tabs look at the settings and think about how you normally work, e.g. when you are selecting text, do you want Word to automatically select whole words? Some people find this useful, some don't.

4   On the **File Locations** tab set the default location for saving your files.

5   On the **Save** tab you can control how you save – notice the **Always create a backup copy** option. Would this be useful, or would most backups just be clutter in your folders?

6   On the **Spelling and Grammar** tab, turn on the **Check spelling as you type** option if you want Word to pick up errors as they occur.

7   Click **OK** to close the dialogue box and save your new settings.

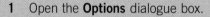
In Word 2002/2003 there is also a Security tab where you can set a password and add other protection.

Now try Assignment 3.3

Module 4

SPREADSHEETS

A spreadsheet (also called a *worksheet*) consists of a grid of cells in which you can write text and numbers, and formulas that can process and analyse that data.

Excel is the leading spreadsheet software. As well as storing and calculating facilities, it offers:

- functions and wizards for perfoming complex calculations and data analysis
- database-style sorting and searching
- full control over the layout and appearance
- easy-to-use graphing routines that can make underlying trends and patterns more visible.

- ◉ Using the computer and managing files
- ◉ Word processing
- ◎ Spreadsheets
- ◎ Databases
- ◎ Presentations
- ◎ Information and communication

 Throughout this unit you will be asked to open files that are supplied in the Resource Bank. They can be found on the Resource Bank CD or in the folder which your tutor may have set up for use with this course.

Basic concepts

Menus and toolbars

Excel has the standard Windows 'look and feel'. You can access all the commands, selecting them with the mouse or with **[Alt]** key combinations. Many commands can be run from toolbars. There are nearly 20, all of which can be turned on or off. Initially only the **Standard** and **Formatting** toolbars are visible. The most used commands are all on these two – notice how many are the same as in Word.

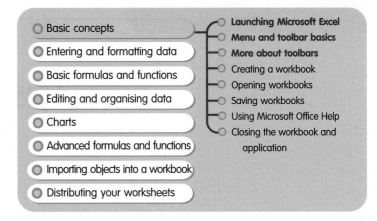

○ Basic concepts

◉ Entering and formatting data

◉ Basic formulas and functions

◉ Editing and organising data

○ Charts

◉ Advanced formulas and functions

◉ Importing objects into a workbook

○ Distributing your worksheets

○ Launching Microsoft Excel
○ Menu and toolbar basics
○ More about toolbars
○ Creating a workbook
○ Opening workbooks
○ Saving workbooks
○ Using Microsoft Office Help
○ Closing the workbook and application

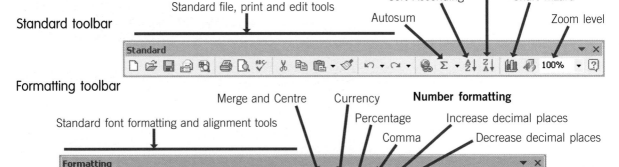

Standard toolbar

Standard file, print and edit tools

Autosum

Sort Ascending

Sort Descending

Chart wizard

Zoom level

Formatting toolbar

Standard font formatting and alignment tools

Merge and Centre

Currency

Percentage

Comma

Number formatting

Increase decimal places

Decrease decimal places

Skill Builder **4.1**

1 Run Excel, either from the **Start** menu or its desktop icon.

2 Open each menu in turn and look through it to see which commands you recognise from other Windows applications.

3 Click on the arrow at the far right of the **Standard** toolbar and select **Show Buttons on One Row**.

4 If you prefer to see more of both toolbars, click the arrow again and select **Show Buttons on Two Rows**.

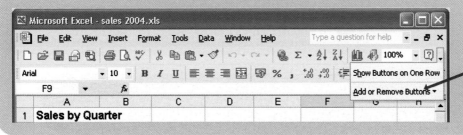

You can choose which toolbar buttons to show

Creating a workbook

An Excel worksheet has 256 columns and 65,536 rows – that's over 16 million cells! You can link any number of worksheets together in a *workbook*. (You are not expected to fill all the cells – the huge space simply means that you can lay out your data any way that you like.)

Each cell is identified by an address, made up from its column letter and row number, e.g. A1 is the top left cell.

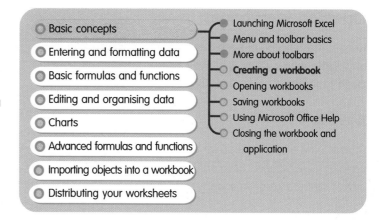

- Basic concepts
- Entering and formatting data
- Basic formulas and functions
- Editing and organising data
- Charts
- Advanced formulas and functions
- Importing objects into a workbook
- Distributing your worksheets

- Launching Microsoft Excel
- Menu and toolbar basics
- More about toolbars
- **Creating a workbook**
- Opening workbooks
- Saving workbooks
- Using Microsoft Office Help
- Closing the workbook and application

To create a new workbook, start with **File > New**, then select a template or the blank workbook.

> Worksheets are also known as spreadsheets, or sheets for short.

Formula bar shows contents of active cell

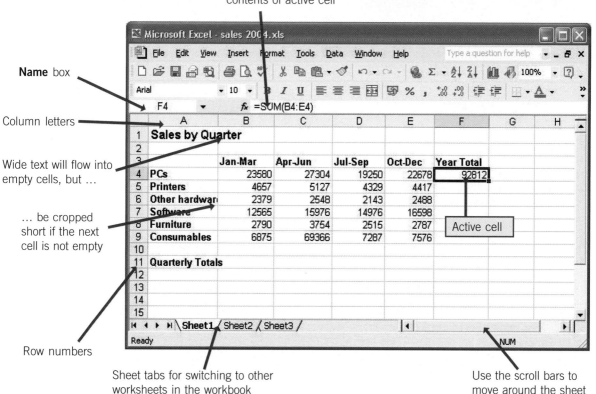

Name box

Column letters

Wide text will flow into empty cells, but …

… be cropped short if the next cell is not empty

Row numbers

Sheet tabs for switching to other worksheets in the workbook

Use the scroll bars to move around the sheet

	A	B	C	D	E	F	G	H
1	Sales by Quarter							
2								
3		Jan-Mar	Apr-Jun	Jul-Sep	Oct-Dec	Year Total		
4	PCs	23580	27304	19250	22678	92812		
5	Printers	4657	5127	4329	4417			
6	Other hardware	2379	2548	2143	2488			
7	Software	12565	15976	14976	16598			
8	Furniture	2790	3754	2515	2787	Active cell		
9	Consumables	6875	69366	7287	7576			
10								
11	Quarterly Totals							
12								
13								
14								
15								

F4 = SUM(B4:E4)

> Worksheets have two layers – the data that you enter in the sheet may not be what you see on the screen or printout. You (normally) see the results of calculations, not the formulas; numbers can be shown in different formats; and the display of text may be cropped short if it is too long to fit into its cell.

Opening workbooks

Recent files can be opened from the end of the **File** menu. Click 📂 or use **File > Open** to find and open older files.

Saving

A lot of time and effort can go into creating a worksheet. Save it early, and save it often to keep your work safe.

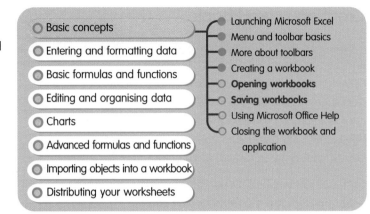

Basic concepts

Entering and formatting data

Basic formulas and functions

Editing and organising data

Charts

Advanced formulas and functions

Importing objects into a workbook

Distributing your worksheets

Launching Microsoft Excel
Menu and toolbar basics
More about toolbars
Creating a workbook
Opening workbooks
Saving workbooks
Using Microsoft Office Help
Closing the workbook and application

Skill Builder **4.2**

1 Click 📂 or use **File > Open** to open *Sales.xls* from the Resource Bank *Module 4* folder.

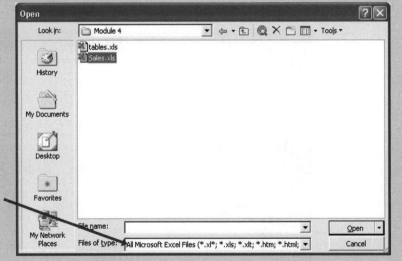

Excel can open or save in different formats, including .csv (comma separated values) the standard format for transferring data between applications

2 Explore the screen, identifying the toolbar buttons and other features covered in the previous two pages.

3 Use **File > Save As** to open the **Save As** dialogue box. Select your work folder to store the file in and save it with the name *MySales*.xls.

Excel Help

There's lots of Help at hand – all you have to do is ask for it. You can ask the Office Assistant, or use the 'Type a question for help' box (in Office XP) or ask the **Answer Wizard** once you have opened the Help system.

Enter key words rather than questions. 'Number format' finds the same Help as 'How do I change the number format?'

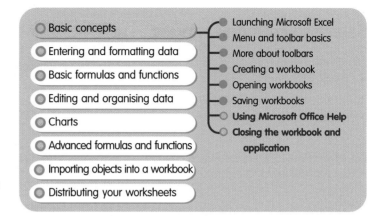

- Basic concepts
- Entering and formatting data
- Basic formulas and functions
- Editing and organising data
- Charts
- Advanced formulas and functions
- Importing objects into a workbook
- Distributing your worksheets

- Launching Microsoft Excel
- Menu and toolbar basics
- More about toolbars
- Creating a workbook
- Opening workbooks
- Saving workbooks
- **Using Microsoft Office Help**
- **Closing the workbook and application**

Skill Builder **4.3**

1 Use the Office Assistant or the 'Type a question for help' box to find Help on selecting cells.

2 If the Help page is not what you want, open the Help window fully and ask the **Answer Wizard**. You will be shown a full list of topics – pick one.

3 Print the Help page. This will be useful at the next stage of this course.

4 Close the Help window.

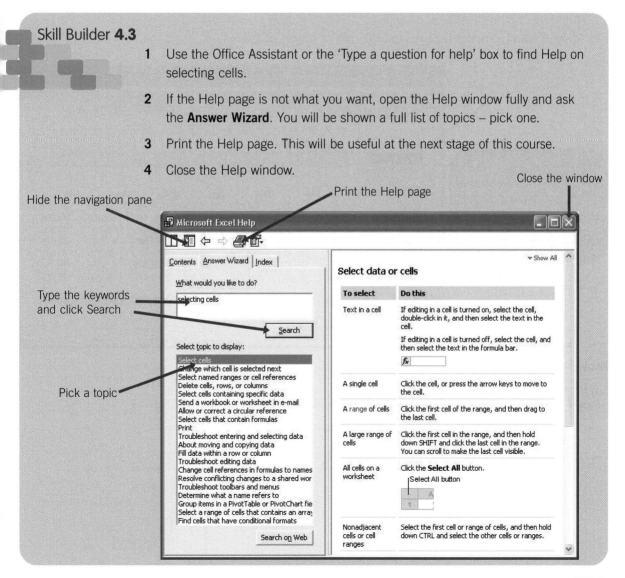

Hide the navigation pane

Print the Help page

Close the window

Type the keywords and click Search

Pick a topic

Entering and formatting data

Selecting cells and ranges

To select:

* a cell, click in it
* a row, click its heading number
* several rows, drag across their numbers
* a column, click its heading letter
* several columns, drag across their letters
* a block, click in one corner, then drag to the opposite corner.

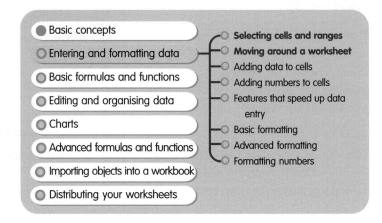

- Basic concepts
- Entering and formatting data
- Basic formulas and functions
- Editing and organising data
- Charts
- Advanced formulas and functions
- Importing objects into a workbook
- Distributing your worksheets

- Selecting cells and ranges
- Moving around a worksheet
- Adding data to cells
- Adding numbers to cells
- Features that speed up data entry
- Basic formatting
- Advanced formatting
- Formatting numbers

Hold down **Control** to select several separate cells or ranges at once.

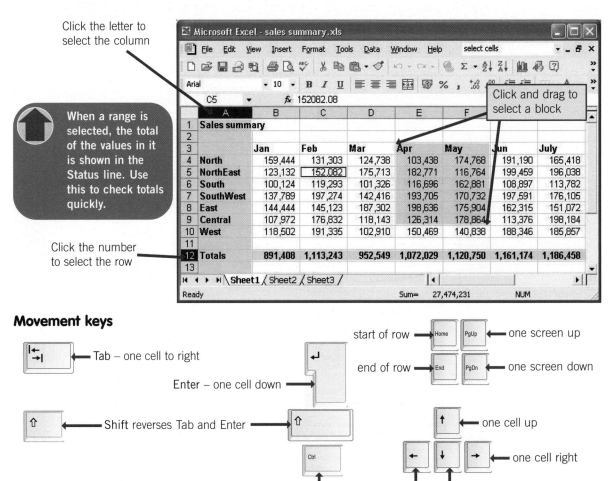

Click the letter to select the column

When a range is selected, the total of the values in it is shown in the Status line. Use this to check totals quickly.

Click the number to select the row

Click and drag to select a block

Movement keys

Tab – one cell to right

Enter – one cell down

Shift reverses Tab and Enter

Hold down to increase effect of movement keys

start of row

end of row

one screen up

one screen down

one cell up

one cell right

one cell down

one cell left

Adding data and numbers

In Excel there are two distinct types of data: text and numbers. When entering data, you do not normally need to tell Excel which type it is – Excel can recognise the difference.

Data can be entered into any cell, so you can lay out text and figures just where you want them. The active cell has a thick border and its address is shown in the **Name** box at the top left.

- ● Basic concepts
  - ○ Selecting cells and ranges
- ○ Entering and formatting data
  - ● Moving around a worksheet
  - **○ Adding data to cells**
- ● Basic formulas and functions
  - **○ Adding numbers to cells**
  - ○ Features that speed up data entry
- ○ Editing and organising data
- ○ Charts
  - ○ Basic formatting
- ○ Advanced formulas and functions
  - ○ Advanced formatting
  - ○ Formatting numbers
- ○ Importing objects into a workbook
- ○ Distributing your worksheets

In this exercise, some of the data in column A is too long to fit in a standard width column and will be displayed cropped short. Don't worry about this. You will learn how to change the column width later in this course.

Skill Builder 4.4

1 Start a new worksheet.

2 Click into cell A1 and type in the title 'Sales by Quarter'.

3 Enter the rest of this data, in the cells indicated, starting with Jan-Mar in B3.

	A	B	C	D	E
1	Sales by Quarter				
2					
3		Jan-Mar	Apr-Jun	Jul-Sep	Oct-Dec
4	PCs	23580	27304	19250	22678
5	Printers	4657	5127	4329	4417
6	Other hardware	2379	2548	2143	2488
7	Software	12565	15976	14976	16598
8	Furniture	2790	3754	2515	2787
9	Consumables	6875	69366	7287	7576
10					
11	Quarterly Totals				

4 Save the file as *quarterly sales.xls*.

Check the numbers as you enter them, and again at the end. Accuracy is as important in ECDL assessments as it is in an office. If you find you have made a mistake, click back into the cell and type the correct value.

Speeding up data entry

AutoFill can create a series from the first one or two entries – Excel just needs enough to identify the series, e.g. a month name or the first two numbers.

AutoComplete will suggest words based on other words in the same column, and on the first few characters that you type. *This doesn't work if there are blank rows in the column.*

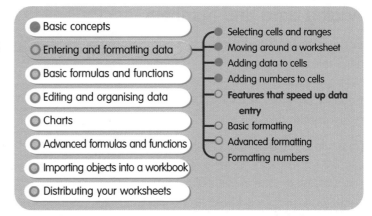

- ● Basic concepts
- ○ Entering and formatting data
- ● Basic formulas and functions
- ○ Editing and organising data
- ○ Charts
- ● Advanced formulas and functions
- ○ Importing objects into a workbook
- ○ Distributing your worksheets

- ● Selecting cells and ranges
- ● Moving around a worksheet
- ● Adding data to cells
- ● Adding numbers to cells
- ○ **Features that speed up data entry**
- ○ Basic formatting
- ○ Advanced formatting
- ○ Formatting numbers

Skill Builder 4.5

1 Start a new workbook.

2 Type the headings into column A as shown here. Autocomplete should spring into action when you start to type headings for the second time.

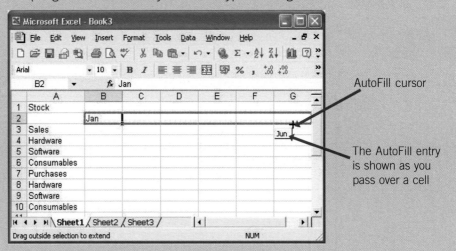

AutoFill cursor

The AutoFill entry is shown as you pass over a cell

3 In B2, type **Jan** and press **[Enter]** or click ☑.

4 Click on B2, point to its lower right corner – the cursor will change to a solid cross – and drag across to G2.

5 Save the file as *stock.xls* and close it.

 If you right-click on a cell and select Pick from list from the shortcut menu, you will be offered a list of the entries already in the same column. Click on an entry to copy it into the cell.

| Consumables |
| Hardware |
| Purchases |
| Sales |
| Software |
| Stock |

Formatting

Text and numbers can be formatted in the same way as in Word, using the tools on the **Formatting** toolbar or the options in the **Format Cells** dialogue box.

There are extra alignment options. **Merge and Centre** take the text in the left cell of a set and centre it across the whole set. You can also set the vertical alignment, display text at an angle, or turn on word-wrap for long items.

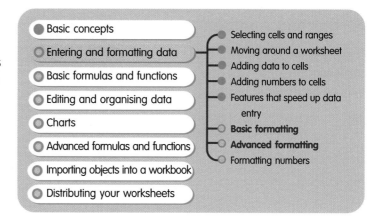

- Basic concepts
  - Selecting cells and ranges
- Entering and formatting data
  - Moving around a worksheet
  - Adding data to cells
- Basic formulas and functions
  - Adding numbers to cells
- Editing and organising data
  - Features that speed up data entry
- Charts
  - **Basic formatting**
- Advanced formulas and functions
  - **Advanced formatting**
- Importing objects into a workbook
  - Formatting numbers
- Distributing your worksheets

Skill Builder **4.6**

1   Open the *quarterly sales* workbook that you saved in Skill Builder 4.4.

2   Select A1 and format it with a serif font, e.g. Times New Roman, size 14.

3   Apply bold to row 3 and column A.

4   Click into cell B2 and type the heading: **Sales excluding VAT**. Make it bold.

5   Merge and centre the heading in B2 across the range B2:E2.

6   Align the headings in row 3 at an angle of 20°.

7   Save the sheet and print one copy.

Merge and Centre

Your spreadsheet should look like this

	A	B	C	D	E	F	G
1	**Sales by Quarter**						
2		**Sales excluding VAT**					
3		*Jan-Mar*	*Apr-Jun*	*Jul-Sep*	*Oct-Dec*		
4	**PCs**	23,580	27,304	19,250	22,678		
5	**Printers**	4,657	5,127	4,329	4,417		
6	**Other hardv**	2,379	2,548	2,143	2,488		
7	**Software**	12,565	15,976	14,976	15,689		
8	**Furniture**	2,790	3,754	2,515	2,787		
9	**Consumabl**	6,875	6,936	7,287	7,576		
10							
11							

Microsoft Excel - quarterly sales.xls

File   Edit   View   Insert   Format   Tools   Data   Window   Help   Type a question for help

Arial   10   **B** *I* U

B2   *fx* Sales excluding VAT

Sheet1 / Sheet2 / Sheet3 /

Ready   NUM

Use these keyboard shortcuts for faster formatting: [Ctrl] + B = Bold on/off; [Ctrl] + I = Italic on/off; [Ctrl] + U = Underline on/off.

Formatting numbers

Numbers can be formatted to help to show what they stand for. The main formats have toolbar buttons:

 Currency, has a £, $ or other money symbol and 2 places of decimals, e.g. £123.45

% Percent, with 0 decimal places and % at the end.

, Comma, with commas every 3 digits and 2 decimal places, e.g. 12,345,678.90

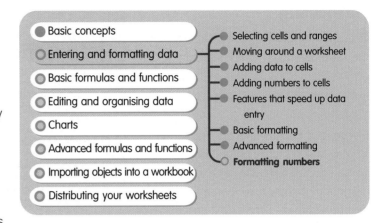

- Basic concepts
- Entering and formatting data
  - Selecting cells and ranges
  - Moving around a worksheet
  - Adding data to cells
  - Adding numbers to cells
  - Features that speed up data entry
  - Basic formatting
  - Advanced formatting
  - **Formatting numbers**
- Basic formulas and functions
- Editing and organising data
- Charts
- Advanced formulas and functions
- Importing objects into a workbook
- Distributing your worksheets

Use ⁺⁰⁰ to increase the decimal places or ⁰⁰⁺ to decrease them. For the full set of formatting options, select the cells, then use Format > Cells to open the Format Cells dialogue box and switch to the Number tab.

Skill Builder 4.7

1 Open the *quarterly sales.xls* workbook, from Skill Builder 4.6.

2 In an unused cell, enter 1234567.89.

3 Select the cell and apply in turn the Currency, Percentage and Comma formats, noting the effect each time. At the end use the command **Edit > Clear > Formats** to remove all formats, then delete the value.

4 Select the range B4:E9. Apply the **Currency** format.

5 Save the sheet and close it.

 If the format makes a number too large to fit in the cell, you will see '##########'. To make the number visible, set a smaller font size or widen the column.

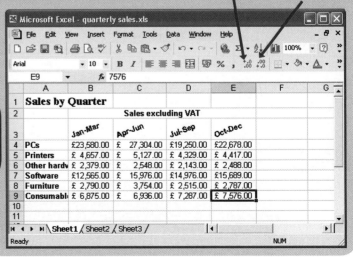

Basic formulas and functions

Simple formulas

A formula starts with an = sign and is made up of *operators* (e.g. +, –, *, /) and *arguments* (the values to be used in the calculations, or the addresses of the cells that hold the values).

When a cell contains a formula, only its result is displayed on screen. If you click into its cell, the formula is displayed in the **Formula** bar.

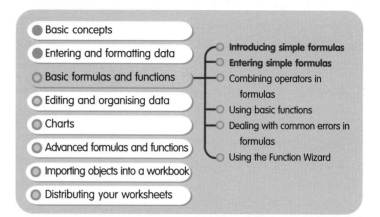

- Basic concepts
- Entering and formatting data
- Basic formulas and functions
  - Introducing simple formulas
  - Entering simple formulas
  - Combining operators in formulas
  - Using basic functions
  - Dealing with common errors in formulas
  - Using the Function Wizard
- Editing and organising data
- Charts
- Advanced formulas and functions
- Importing objects into a workbook
- Distributing your worksheets

Skill Builder 4.8

1 Open your *quarterly sales.xls* workbook.

2 Edit the heading in A1 to read 'Sales'.

3 Adjust the width of column A so that all its data is visible.

4 In F3, type the heading 'Year Totals'. Format it to match the other headings.

5 In F4, enter a formula to find the total value of PC sales, starting = B4+C4…

6 Write similar formula to find the other year totals, in F5, F6, F7, F8 and F9.

7 Save the edited workbook.

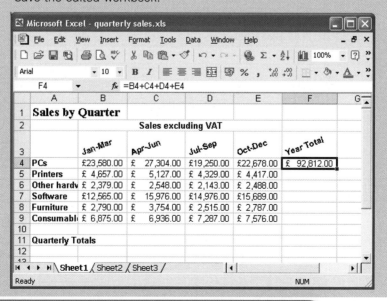

When writing a formula you can type a cell address, or click into the cell – Excel will write the address into the formula for you.

Combining operators

If a formula has more than one operator, calculations are performed left to right, in the order of the **BODMAS** rules.

Brackets – e.g. $(2 + 4) * 3 = 18$
Of – power of, e.g. $3^2 = 9$
Division
Multiplication
Addition
Subtraction

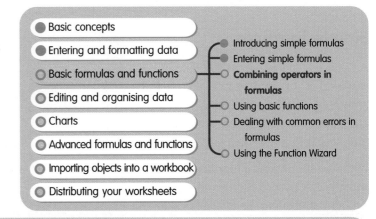

- Basic concepts
- Entering and formatting data
- Basic formulas and functions
- Editing and organising data
- Charts
- Advanced formulas and functions
- Importing objects into a workbook
- Distributing your worksheets

- Introducing simple formulas
- Entering simple formulas
- **Combining operators in formulas**
- Using basic functions
- Dealing with common errors in formulas
- Using the Function Wizard

Skill Builder **4.9**

In this exercise you will work out the final marks for students, based on two essays (out of 10 and 15) and a written exam (out of 50). To get a final mark, you add the essay marks, multiply the result by 2 then add the exam mark.

1 Start a new workbook and enter this data in the cells indicated.

	A	B	C	D	E
1	End of year marks				
2					
3	Student	Essay 1	Essay 2	Exam	Final
4		Marks /10	Marks /15	Marks /50	Score /100
5	Alice Atkins	8	12	32	
6	Brian Brown	6	9	21	
7	Carol Chang	7	13	38	
8	David Davies	9	10	26	

2 Write a formula in E5 to add B5 and C5, multiply the result by 2 then add D5.

3 Write similar formulas in cells E6 to E8.

4 Save the workbook as *marks.xls*.

Your worksheet should look like this

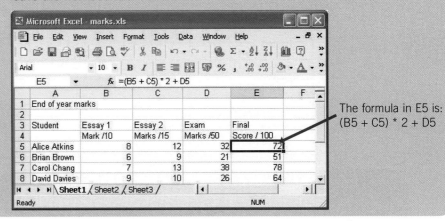

The formula in E5 is:
$(B5 + C5) * 2 + D5$

Using basic functions

As well as the arithmetic operators, formulas may contain functions – ready-made calculations.

The simplest function is SUM(*range*) which gives the total of the values held in the *range*. e.g. =SUM(B4:B12) gives the total of the values held in the cells from B4 down to B12.

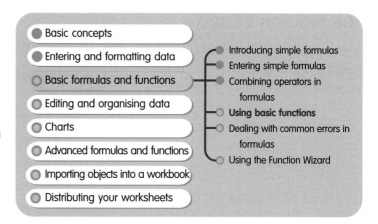

- Basic concepts
- Entering and formatting data
- Basic formulas and functions
  - Introducing simple formulas
  - Entering simple formulas
  - Combining operators in formulas
  - **Using basic functions**
  - Dealing with common errors in formulas
  - Using the Function Wizard
- Editing and organising data
- Charts
- Advanced formulas and functions
- Importing objects into a workbook
- Distributing your worksheets

AutoSum

The AutoSum tool offers a quick way to create a formula using SUM(). Select the range of cells you want to add and a blank cell below or to the right and click Σ.

AutoFill and formulas

If you click on a cell containing a formula and drag into adjacent cells, the formula will be copied into those cells. As it is copied the cell references in the formulas will be adjusted so that they continue to refer to the same relative cells. For example, if C1 contained = A1 + B1, when copied into C2 the formula would read =A2 + B2.

Skill Builder 4.10

1　Open your *quarterly sales.xls* workbook.

2　In B11 enter this formula to find the Jan–Mar total: = SUM(B4:B10).

3　Use AutoFill to copy the formula into C10, D10 and E10.

4　Save the file.

Here's a quick way to find the total of a range. Select the range and the blank cell below it or to its right where the formula is to go, then click **AutoSUM**.

If you leave an extra blank line between the range and its total, you can insert more lines later and the range in the formula will expand automatically

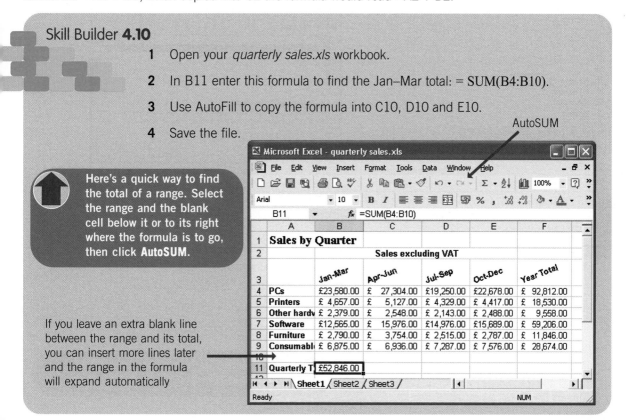

The Function Wizard

In Excel 2002 and later, the **Paste Function** tool is replaced by the **Insert Function** button on the Formula Bar. Apart from the change of name, and a slightly different layout to the dialogue box, things are the same as before.

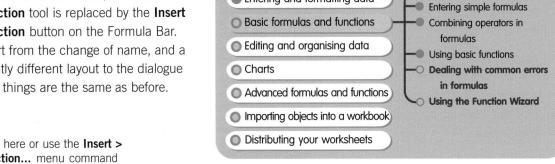

- Basic concepts
- Entering and formatting data
- Basic formulas and functions
  - Introducing simple formulas
  - Entering simple formulas
  - Combining operators in formulas
  - Using basic functions
  - **Dealing with common errors in formulas**
  - **Using the Function Wizard**
- Editing and organising data
- Charts
- Advanced formulas and functions
- Importing objects into a workbook
- Distributing your worksheets

Click here or use the **Insert > Function...** menu command

Click to drop down the category list

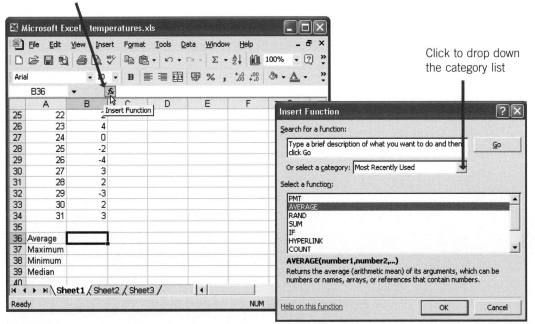

Skill Builder 4.11

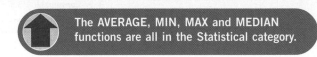

1   Open the *temperatures.xls* workbook from the Resource Bank *Module 4* folder. It has temperature readings for January in cells B4 to B34.

2   Use functions to find the average, minimum, maximum and median values. (There are labels already in place in cells A36 to A39.)

3   Save the file in your work folder.

The **AVERAGE, MIN, MAX** and **MEDIAN** functions are all in the Statistical category.

66

Editing and organising data

Editing

You can get into a cell and edit its contents, but it can sometimes be quicker to retype the data.

Editing an Excel cell

Click once into the cell to select it and its contents. If you type anything now, this will replace the contents; pressing **[Backspace]** or **[Delete]** will erase the contents.

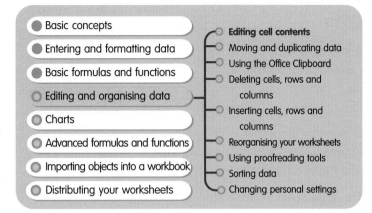

- Basic concepts
- Entering and formatting data
- Basic formulas and functions
- Editing and organising data
- Charts
- Advanced formulas and functions
- Importing objects into a workbook
- Distributing your worksheets

  - Editing cell contents
  - Moving and duplicating data
  - Using the Office Clipboard
  - Deleting cells, rows and columns
  - Inserting cells, rows and columns
  - Reorganising your worksheets
  - Using proofreading tools
  - Sorting data
  - Changing personal settings

Double-click into a cell to put it into edit mode. You can now edit the contents.

- ◆ Press **[Backspace]** or **[Delete]** to erase errors
- ◆ Use the **[←]** and **[→]** keys to move the cursor
- ◆ Type in new data as needed
- ◆ Click Enter ☑ or Cancel ☒ when you have finished editing.

Skill Builder **4.12**

1 Open the *quarterly sales* workbook.

2 Replace the current value for Software, Oct–Dec (E7) with this: 15689

3 Edit the value for Consumables in Apr–Jun (C9) to read 6936.

4 Save the edited sheet, then close it.

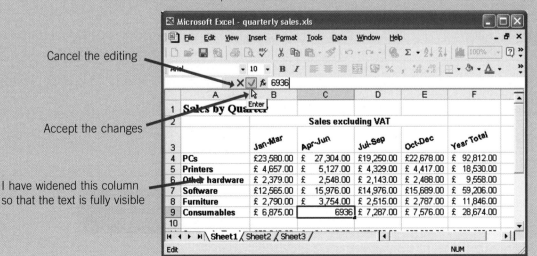

Cancel the editing

Accept the changes

I have widened this column so that the text is fully visible

Moving and duplicating data

The drag method is good for moving or copying data or formulas into adjacent cells, but is no use for moving or copying to a different part of the sheet.

If you want to move or copy a single cell or range, then the standard **Cut**, **Copy** and **Paste** commands work very well.

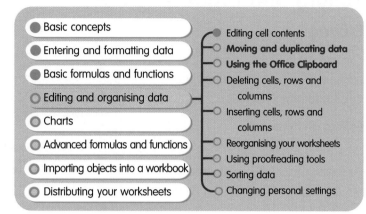

- ● Basic concepts
- ● Entering and formatting data
- ● Basic formulas and functions
- ○ Editing and organising data
- ● Charts
- ● Advanced formulas and functions
- ● Importing objects into a workbook
- ○ Distributing your worksheets

- ● Editing cell contents
- ○ **Moving and duplicating data**
- ○ **Using the Office Clipboard**
- ○ Deleting cells, rows and columns
- ○ Inserting cells, rows and columns
- ○ Reorganising your worksheets
- ○ Using proofreading tools
- ○ Sorting data
- ○ Changing personal settings

The Clipboard

The Office Clipboard allows you to cut or copy up to 12 (24 in the XP version) separate cells, ranges or data from other Office applications, and paste any one of them – or all of them – into a new location.

To paste an item, click where it is to go, then click on the item

To remove an item from the Clipboard, click on the arrow on its right and select **Delete**

 In Office XP, the Clipboard is a Task Pane option, not a toolbar. You may need to display it first before you can cut or copy into it.

Skill Builder **4.13**

1 Open the *temperatures.xls* workbook from the *Module 4* folder.

2 It has temperature readings for February in column H and for March in column N. Move these so that the data is in columns C and D.

3 Copy your new formulas for January, (in cells B36 to B39) and apply them to the values for February and March.

4 Save the file in your work folder.

 The **Edit > Paste Special** menu command gives you a range of options for copying data. Explore them.

Deleting rows and columns

If you select a row, column or any range of cells and press **[Delete]**, the contents of the cells are deleted, but the cells themselves remain in place. Sometimes you need to remove unwanted cells completely to restructure a sheet. When a row or column is removed, the remaining rows (columns) move up (left) to fill the gap.

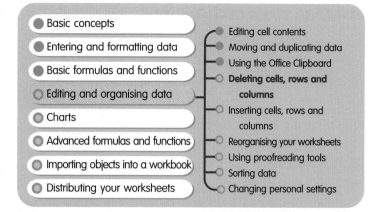

- Basic concepts
- Entering and formatting data
- Basic formulas and functions
- Editing and organising data
- Charts
- Advanced formulas and functions
- Importing objects into a workbook
- Distributing your worksheets

- Editing cell contents
- Moving and duplicating data
- Using the Office Clipboard
- **Deleting cells, rows and columns**
- Inserting cells, rows and columns
- Reorganising your worksheets
- Using proofreading tools
- Sorting data
- Changing personal settings

Skill Builder **4.14**

1 Open the *salaries.xls* workbook from the Resource Bank *Module 4* folder.

2 Moira Reid has left the company. Delete her data from the sheet.

   Select the row (7), then open the **View** menu and select **Delete**, or right-click on the row and select **Delete**.

3 Sorry, that was a mistake. Moira is still with the company. Click ↻ ▾ or use **Edit > Undo** to restore her data.

4 John White has left the company. Delete his data from the sheet.

5 Save the sheet in your work folder.

> Before deleting rows or columns, look across or down the sheet to check that there is nothing you need further along those rows or columns.

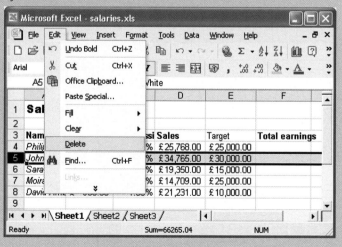

> You can 'fold' the sheet to hide rows or columns that contain sensitive data, or details that are necessary for your formulas but which clutter the display. To hide the column, select it and use **Format > Column > Hide** or right-click on it and select **Hide** from the shortcut menu. To unhide a column. Select the ones on either side of the hidden one then right-click and select **Unhide**, or use **Format > Column > Unhide**.

Inserting rows and columns

Rows and columns can be inserted into your work area. Existing rows and columns will move down or to the right to make room.

Any formatting already applied to cells either side of the inserted ones will be applied to the new cells.

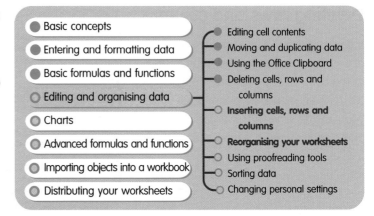

- Basic concepts
- Entering and formatting data
- Basic formulas and functions
- Editing and organising data
- Charts
- Advanced formulas and functions
- Importing objects into a workbook
- Distributing your worksheets

- Editing cell contents
- Moving and duplicating data
- Using the Office Clipboard
- Deleting cells, rows and columns
- **Inserting cells, rows and columns**
- **Reorganising your worksheets**
- Using proofreading tools
- Sorting data
- Changing personal settings

Skill Builder **4.15**

1   Open the copy of *salaries.xls* that you saved in Skill Builder 4.14.

2   Insert two rows below row 4.

3   Enter the data given here inthe new rows 5 and 6:

	A	B	C	D	E
5	Wendy Kroy	1,750	4%	39,860	30000
6	Bill Pullman	1,400	3%	22,867	27500

4   The formatting should be the same as on the rows above and below. If it is not, format the cells to match the other rows.

5   Print one copy of the sheet, save and close it.

Your sheet should now look like this

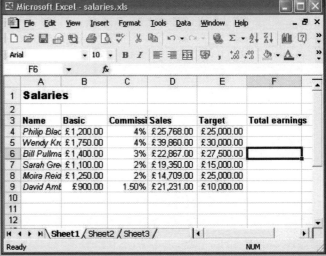

The simplest way to reorganise a workbook, is to use the menu that opens when you right-click on a sheet tab.

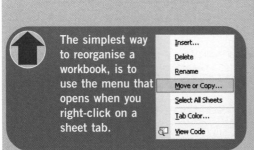

Proofreading

Accuracy in spreadsheets is essential – in ECDL assessments and in life! Always check your data and formulas. The spell checker will pick up most typing errors. Don't forget to use it.

Use **Find** to locate data – the larger the sheet, the more useful this tool is.

Use **Replace** to find and replace several occurrences of a text item.

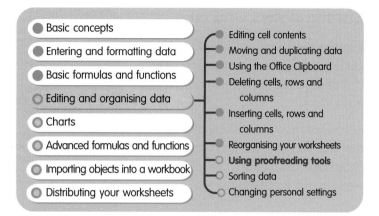

- Basic concepts
  - Editing cell contents
  - Moving and duplicating data
  - Using the Office Clipboard
  - Deleting cells, rows and columns
  - Inserting cells, rows and columns
- Entering and formatting data
- Basic formulas and functions
- Editing and organising data
  - Reorganising your worksheets
  - **Using proofreading tools**
  - Sorting data
- Charts
- Advanced formulas and functions
- Importing objects into a workbook
- Distributing your worksheets
  - Changing personal settings

Skill Builder **4.16**

1 Open the *stationery.xls* workbook from the Resource Bank *Module 4* folder.

2 Run the spell check on it. Notice that product names, may not be recognised, and that words may be spelled correctly, but misused. Read the sheet, before and after the spell check.

3 The biros are 'Click' not 'Bic'. Use **Replace** to change all the entries.

4 To save time at data entry, the abreviation 'RS' was used instead of typing out 'Railway Stationers' in full. Use **Replace** to change it – and turn on the Match case option first. Why?

5 Save the edited file in your work folder.

The edited worksheet should look like this

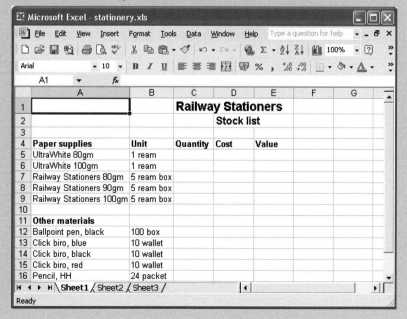

Sorting data

Excel can sort a list or table of data into alphabetic, numeric or date order. We can use the salaries workbook to explore this feature.

Remember that for anything other than the simplest sorts, you should select the data block – including its headings – then use the **Sort Data** dialogue box.

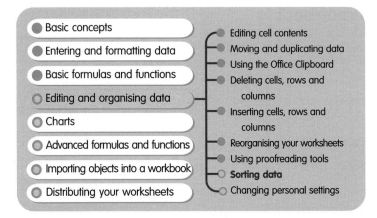

- Basic concepts
- Entering and formatting data
- Basic formulas and functions
- Editing and organising data
- Charts
- Advanced formulas and functions
- Importing objects into a workbook
- Distributing your worksheets

- Editing cell contents
- Moving and duplicating data
- Using the Office Clipboard
- Deleting cells, rows and columns
- Inserting cells, rows and columns
- Reorganising your worksheets
- Using proofreading tools
- **Sorting data**
- Changing personal settings

Skill Builder **4.17**

1 Open the copy of *salaries.xls* that you saved in Skill Builder 4.15.

2 Sort the table of data into ascending order of **Sales**.

3 Sort the table into descending order of **Commission**, then into descending order of **Basic**.

Your sheet should now look like this

	A	B	C	D	E	F	G
1	**Salaries**						
2							
3	**Name**	**Basic**	**Commission**	**Sales**	**Target**	**Total earnings**	
4	Wendy Kroy	£1,750.00	4%	£39,860.00	£30,000.00		
5	Philip Black	£1,200.00	4%	£25,768.00	£25,000.00		
6	Bill Pullman	£1,400.00	3%	£22,867.00	£27,500.00		
7	Moira Reid	£1,250.00	2%	£14,709.00	£25,000.00		
8	Sarah Grey	£1,100.00	2%	£19,350.00	£15,000.00		
9	David Ambrose	£ 900.00	1.50%	£21,231.00	£10,000.00		
10							
11							

4 Sort the table of data into ascending order of **Name**. What would we have to do to get David Ambrose at the top of the list and Moira Reid at the end?

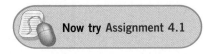

Now try Assignment 4.1

Charts

What is a chart?

Charts can help to reveal the patterns in sets of numbers. They can make it easier to compare the sizes of values, bring out trends as values change over time, and highlight the relationships between values.

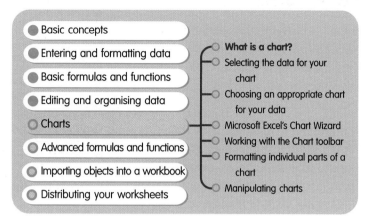

Charting terms

A **data point** is a value plotted in a graph.

A **data series** is a set of data points that would have been in one row, or one column in the spreadsheet. They will be shown as one line or a set of bars in the chart.

The **legend** shows the labels for the data series.

The **Category** or **X axis** lies at the bottom of the chart – if the data shows change over time, time usually occupies this axis. The **Value** or **Y axis** runs up the side.

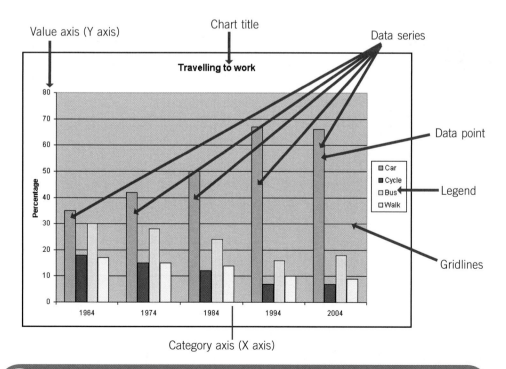

 'Graph' or 'chart'? We normally use 'graph' where values are shown as lines, and 'chart' where they are shown as blocks of colour or shading.

Selecting data for a chart

If the chart data is in a solid block with headings above and to the side, then creating a chart is simple. If the data is not so organised, you must first select the rows or columns to use.

If the data is in rows, i.e. each row will form a series, the top headings will be used to label the Category axis of the chart, and the side headings will be used to label the series in the legend. If the data is in columns, the headings will be used the other way round.

- Basic concepts
- Entering and formatting data
- Basic formulas and functions
- Editing and organising data
- Charts
- Advanced formulas and functions
- Importing objects into a workbook
- Distributing your worksheets

- What is a chart?
- **Selecting the data for your chart**
- Choosing an appropriate chart for your data
- Microsoft Excel's Chart Wizard
- Working with the Chart toolbar
- Formatting individual parts of a chart
- Manipulating charts

Skill Builder **4.18**

The first job is to create a table of data suitable for graphing.

1 Start a new workbook.

2 Enter the following data, in the cells indicated.

	A	B	C	D	E	F
1	Travelling to work					
2						
3		1964	1974	1984	1994	2004
4	Car	35	42	50	67	66
5	Cycle	18	15	12	7	7
6	Bus	30	28	24	16	18
7	Walk	17	15	14	10	9

3 Save the workbook as *travel.xls* in your work folder.

If you were creating a chart to compare all modes of travel across all five years, you would start by selecting the whole data table, A3:F7.

This screenshot shows the data being selected to make a pie chart. The data series is in F4:F7, with its heading in F3, and the labels are in A3:A7. To select two or more separate rows or columns, hold down **[Ctrl]** while you select.

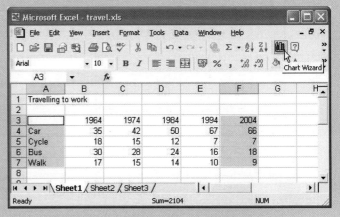

Choosing an appropriate chart

Graphs and charts can show changes over time, variations between areas, the relative contribution that the parts make to a whole, and other relationships between numbers. There are different types of graphs, designed to bring out different kinds of relationships. The three most commonly used types are: bar charts, line graphs and pie charts.

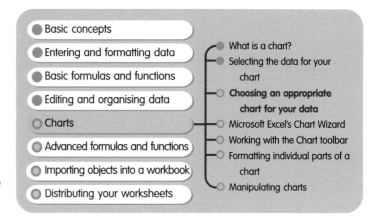

- Basic concepts
- Entering and formatting data
- Basic formulas and functions
- Editing and organising data
- Charts
- Advanced formulas and functions
- Importing objects into a workbook
- Distributing your worksheets

- What is a chart?
- Selecting the data for your chart
- **Choosing an appropriate chart for your data**
- Microsoft Excel's Chart Wizard
- Working with the Chart toolbar
- Formatting individual parts of a chart
- Manipulating charts

Bar charts

Bar charts are good for comparing several series of data – and especially for comparing the figures at the same point in the series. In this example, you can see that more people have travelled by car than by any other means of transport over the whole time of this chart, and that the bus has always been the second most used means.

The bars can run either vertically or horizontally. In Excel, vertical bar charts are called column charts.

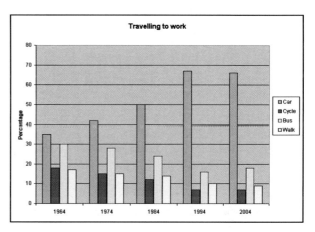

Line graphs

Line graphs are used for comparing several series, where you want to show changes over time. Here, for example, we can see that car use rose rapidly between 1964 and 1994, but that it has fallen off slightly since then.

Line graphs show trends and can be useful when trying to forecast numbers – the eye can follow the direction of the line. They also enable you to estimate values between data points. Here, if you wanted an idea of the car use in 1990, you could draw a line up from the X axis and see where it crossed the car line.

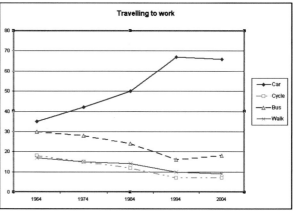

Pie charts

A pie chart can only display one series at a time, but it does show the relative contribution of each figure to the total. Here we can see that in 2004, around twice as many people travelled by car as by all the other modes put together.

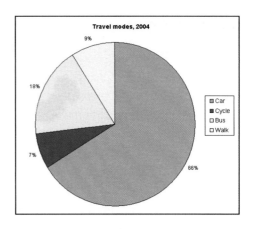

Combination charts

Different types of display can be combined in the same chart. For example, lines are often drawn on bar charts to emphasise trends. Excel offers ready made line and column combinations in its **Custom Types** set, and you can easily add a trendline on any bar chart – it's an option on the shortcut menu.

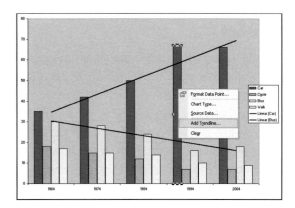

Type variations and format options

Every type of chart has many variations, and some of these may be better than others for bringing out the meaning of the data. The colours and fill effects of pie slices and bars, and the size, style and postion of text items can all add to the impact and readability of charts.

But try not to overdo it. This 3-D exploded pie chart with its textured and gradient shaded fills may be visually striking, but does it tell you any more than the simpler 2-D version at the top of this page, and would you want to look at it for very long?

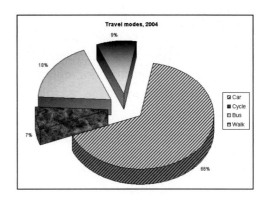

The Chart Wizard

In Excel the **Chart Wizard** is the only way to create charts, and the simplest way to format them. Many of the options and settings can be changed later, if required.

The Wizard has four steps, with options at each step. The main options and settings are summarised here.

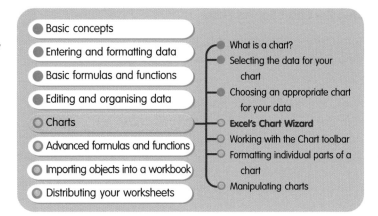

- ● Basic concepts
- ● Entering and formatting data
- ● Basic formulas and functions
- ● Editing and organising data
- ○ Charts
- ● Advanced formulas and functions
- ● Importing objects into a workbook
- ● Distributing your worksheets

- ● What is a chart?
- ● Selecting the data for your chart
- ● Choosing an appropriate chart for your data
- ◉ **Excel's Chart Wizard**
- ○ Working with the Chart toolbar
- ○ Formatting individual parts of a chart
- ○ Manipulating charts

Starting the Wizard

The key to success in using the Wizard is to make sure that you select the data for the series and labels before you start.

Click the **Chart Wizard** button on the **Standard** toolbar to begin.

Chart Wizard

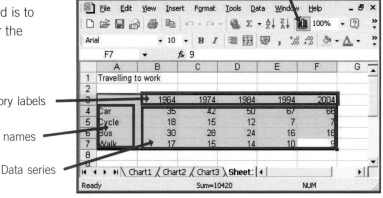

Category labels
Series names
Data series

Step 1 – Chart Type

The **Wizard** can produce a dozen types of chart, with lots of variations in each type. Select the type from the list on the left, then the sub-type from the display on the right.

Use the **Press and Hold to View Sample** button if you want to know how the selected type will work with your data.

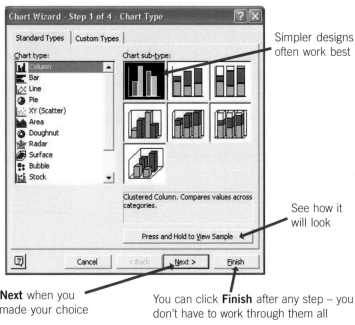

Simpler designs often work best

See how it will look

Click **Next** when you have made your choice

You can click **Finish** after any step – you don't have to work through them all

Step 2 – Chart Source Data

You will have chosen the data table before you started the Wizard, but if you need to change it, you can do so here.

Where there are several data series, Excel assumes that they are in rows. If the series are in columns, change the setting at this step.

Check the sample – if it looks wrong, check the **Data range** and the **Rows/Columns** setting

Data in columns?

At every step, you can go back to earlier steps to change the settings

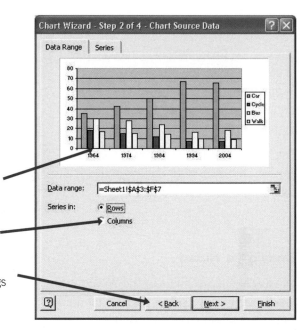

Step 3 – Chart Options

The options vary a little, depending upon the type of chart – there can never be gridlines on a pie chart, for example – and some options have very specialised uses.

Click to bring the tab to the front

On the **Titles** tab, you can type a title for the chart itself, and titles for the X and Y axes. You would almost always have the chart and X axis title. The Y axis title is often missed out if its meaning is obvious.

The **Axes** tab is normally only used if you have a second axis, so that one or more data series can be plotted on a different scale to the rest. This is not required in New CLAIT.

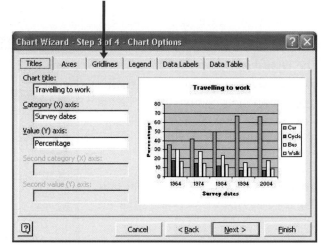

On the **Gridlines** tab, you can turn the gridlines on or off for both axes. Y gridlines make it easier to estimate the values of bars. Both X and Y gridlines are needed on a line graph if you want to be able to read in-between values accurately.

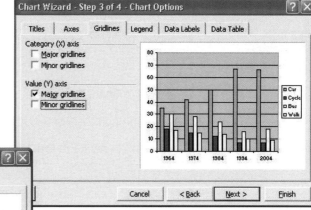

Use the **Legend** tab to set the position of the Legend. Clear the tick from the **Show Legend** box if it is not wanted.

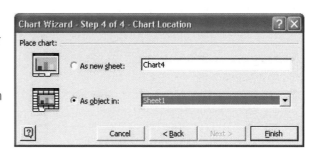

Go to the **Data Labels** tab if you want to display values or other information beside each data point. Data labels are often added to pie charts, but are not normally displayed on bar charts or line graphs.

If the chart is to be displayed in its own sheet (see below), and you want to show the data on which it is based, go to the **Data Table** tab and turn on the **Show data table** option.

Step 4 – Chart Location

A chart can be placed on its own separate sheet, or embedded in a worksheet. Use a separate sheet if you want to be able to print the chart by itself, using the full sheet of paper. Place it as an object in the sheet if you want to keep it close to its data.

Skill Builder **4.19**

1 Open the *travel.xls* workbook that you created in Skill Builder 4.18.

2 Select the whole data table, along with the headers (A3:F7).

3 Click the **Chart Wizard** tool.

4 Work through the Wizard. At Step 1, **Chart Type**, select **Column**.

5 At Step 2, check the **Data range** and correct it if necessary. Make sure the **Series** are in **Rows**.

6 At Step 3, enter Travelling to work as the **Chart title**, Percentage as the **Y axis title** and Survey dates as the **X axis title**.

7 At Step 4, place the chart as an object in the same sheet as the data.

8 Click **Finish**.

9 Save the workbook.

The top left cell is usually empty

Notice that when the chart is selected, the cells containing its data and headings are highlighted

Your worksheet and chart should look like this – the size of the chart will depend upon the size of the window

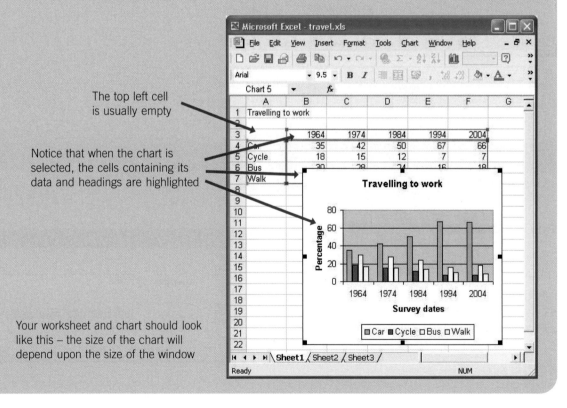

The Chart toolbar

When a chart is first placed in a sheet, or when it is selected again later, the **Chart** toolbar should appear. (If it does not, right-click on any toolbar and place a tick beside **Chart**.)

The toolbar has a small but useful set of tools for accessing chart objects and for setting some options.

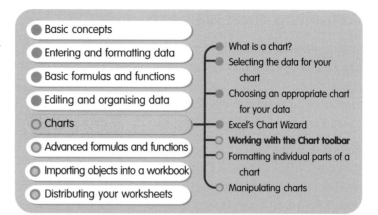

- ● Basic concepts
- ● Entering and formatting data
- ● Basic formulas and functions
- ● Editing and organising data
- ○ Charts
- ● Advanced formulas and functions
- ● Importing objects into a workbook
- ● Distributing your worksheets

- ● What is a chart?
- ● Selecting the data for your chart
- ● Choosing an appropriate chart for your data
- ● Excel's Chart Wizard
- ● **Working with the Chart toolbar**
- ○ Formatting individual parts of a chart
- ○ Manipulating charts

Skill Builder **4.20**

1 Open the *travel.xls* workbook from Skill Builder 4.19 and arrange the window so that you can see the chart clearly.

2 Click on the legend to select it.

3 Use the **Chart** toolbar button to turn the legend off.

4 Use the **Chart** toolbar to select the category axis.

5 Set the category axis headings to 45° up.

6 Save the workbook.

Your sheet and chart should look like this

Chart object – select from the list

Open Format dialogue box

Legend on/off

Headings at 45° down

Series in rows

Chart type

Data table on/off

Series in columns

Headings at 45° up

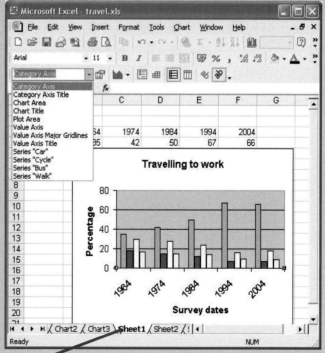

If there are several sheets in a workbook, click on a tab to bring its sheet to the front

Formatting chart elements

The appearance of any chart element can be changed through its **Format** dialogue box. Open this from the **Chart** toolbar, or right-click on the object and select **Format** from its shortcut menu.

Format dialogue boxes vary according to the object. They all have a **Pattern** tab for setting the pattern and colour. Titles have a **Font** tab; values have a **Number** tab. These are used in the same way as elsewhere on the sheet.

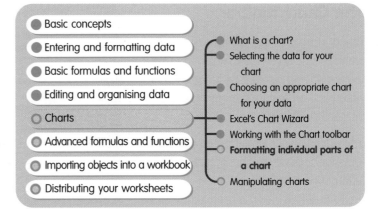

- Basic concepts
- Entering and formatting data
- Basic formulas and functions
- Editing and organising data
- Charts
- Advanced formulas and functions
- Importing objects into a workbook
- Distributing your worksheets

- What is a chart?
- Selecting the data for your chart
- Choosing an appropriate chart for your data
- Excel's Chart Wizard
- Working with the Chart toolbar
- **Formatting individual parts of a chart**
- Manipulating charts

 Before you can format anything, you must select it. Selecting data series and points can be tricky. To select a series (a set of bars, a line or the pie), click once anywhere on it. To select a data point, click twice on the bar, point or slice.

Skill Builder 4.21

1 Open the *travel.xls* workbook from the previous Skill Builder.

2 Create a pie chart based on the figures for 2004. Title it 'Travel modes, 2004'. Display Percentages as the Data Labels. Place the chart in its own sheet.

3 Select each of the slices in turn to open the **Format Data Point** dialogue box. Set a different colour or pattern for each slice to make them stand out more.

4 Change the chart area (background) colour to pale yellow.

5 Save the workbook.

Your chart should look something like this, but with your own fill patterns and colours – I have just selected a slice and am about to reformat it

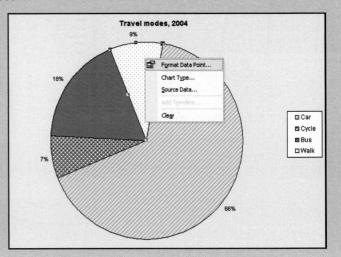

Manipulating a chart

When a chart is placed in a sheet, it is often the wrong size and in the wrong place. This is easily corrected.

Click anywhere on the background to select the chart. You can then drag to move it, or drag on its handles to resize.

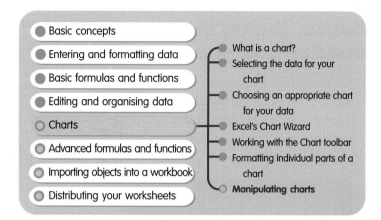

Skill Builder 4.22

1 Locate the bar chart embedded in the sheet in *travel.xls*.

2 Resize the chart so that it is around 6 columns wide and 16 rows high.

3 Move the chart so that its top left corner is on cell B8.

4 Adjust the Y axis scale, setting the Maximum to 70 and the Minor Unit to 5, and turn the minor Y axis gridlines on.

5 Set the category axis headings back to horizontal.

6 Resave the file.

On the **Scale** tab of the **Format Axis** dialogue box, you can set your own values for the Y axis, e.g. if all the values are high, you may want to raise the minimum from the default 0.

Click on the background to select and drag to move

Drag to resize

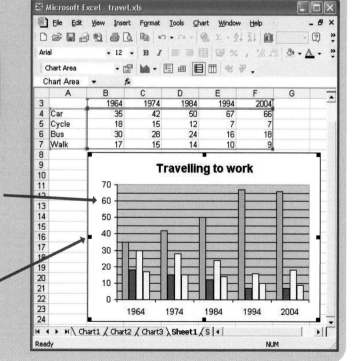

Now try Assignment 4.2

83

Advanced formulas and functions

Relative, absolute and mixed cell addresses

When formulas are duplicated, cell references are usually adjusted relative to the new position. You can fix the column or row or both parts of a reference, so that it does not change.

When writing a formula, click the cell to get the reference, then press **[F4]** to cycle through the absolute and mixed alternatives, e.g. B4, B$4, $B4, B4.

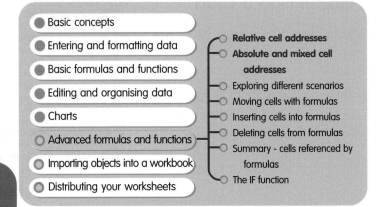

- ● Basic concepts
- ● Entering and formatting data
- ● Basic formulas and functions
- ● Editing and organising data
- ● Charts
- ○ Advanced formulas and functions
- ○ Importing objects into a workbook
- ○ Distributing your worksheets

  - ○ Relative cell addresses
  - ○ Absolute and mixed cell addresses
  - ○ Exploring different scenarios
  - ○ Moving cells with formulas
  - ○ Inserting cells into formulas
  - ○ Deleting cells from formulas
  - ○ Summary - cells referenced by formulas
  - ○ The IF function

Skill Builder **4.23**

1 Start a new worksheet.

2 Enter the headings in A1 and row 3, as shown below.

3 If you can, find the current exchange rates for the pound with the euro, US dollar, Hong Kong dollar and Japanese yen. If not, use the values shown. Enter these into cells B4 to E4.

4 Enter the values 10,20,30…100 in the range A5 to A14.

5 Create a formula in B5 to multiply the value in A5 (fixing the column) with the exchange rate in B4 (fixing the row).

6 Copy the B5 formula into the whole range B5:E14.

The finished worksheet should look something like this

Microsoft Excel - currency.xls

B5 = =$A5*B$4

	A	B	C	D	E	F
1	**Currency conversion**					
2						
3	**£**	**Euro**	**US Dollar**	**HK Dollar**	**Yen**	
4	**Today's rates**	**1.38**	**1.8**	**14.07**	**190.86**	
5	10	13.80	18.00	140.70	1,908.60	
6	20	27.60	36.00	281.40	3,817.20	
7	30	41.40	54.00	422.10	5,725.80	
8	40	55.20	72.00	562.80	7,634.40	
9	50	69.00	90.00	703.50	9,543.00	
10	60	82.80	108.00	844.20	11,451.60	
11	70	96.60	126.00	984.90	13,360.20	
12	80	110.40	144.00	1,125.60	15,268.80	
13	90	124.20	162.00	1,266.30	17,177.40	
14	100	138.00	180.00	1,407.00	19,086.00	

Sheet1 / Sheet2 / Sheet3 /

Ready

Exploring different scenarios

Even the largest and most complex spreadsheet can be recalculated in a few seconds, which allows us to try out different scenarios and see what would happen in different futures.

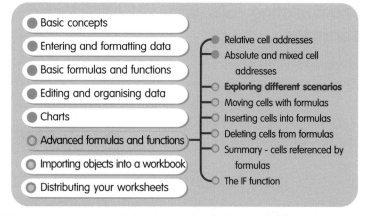

- Basic concepts
- Entering and formatting data
- Basic formulas and functions
- Editing and organising data
- Charts
- Advanced formulas and functions
- Importing objects into a workbook
- Distributing your worksheets

  - Relative cell addresses
  - Absolute and mixed cell addresses
  - **Exploring different scenarios**
  - Moving cells with formulas
  - Inserting cells into formulas
  - Deleting cells from formulas
  - Summary - cells referenced by formulas
  - The IF function

Skill Builder **4.24**

1 Open the *scenario.xls* worksheet in the Resource Bank *Module 4* folder.

2 What would be the profit in Year 5 if the rate of increase was 10% (enter 1.1 in B3)? What would it be if the rate of increase was 200%?

3 Format the cells so that the start and end cells of the what-if? calculations (i.e., B3, F5 and F10) stand out. Make the headings bold, and set the *Profit/Loss* values in a different colour.

4 The *Production costs* and *Fixed costs* figures are also produced by formulas. Turn on the display of formulas so that you can see them.

5 Rewrite the formulas so that *Production costs* are set at 60% of Sales, and so that *Fixed costs* rise by only 5% (1.05) each year.

6 Save the sheet in your work folder.

The finished worksheet should look something like this

> Never forget that all 'What if?' calculations are based on guesses.

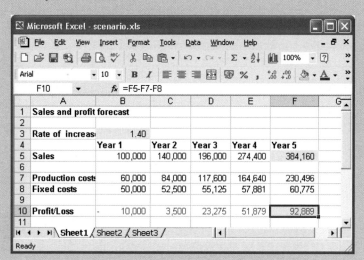

Microsoft Excel - scenario.xls

F10 =F5-F7-F8

	A	B	C	D	E	F	G
1	Sales and profit forecast						
2							
3	Rate of increas	1.40					
4		Year 1	Year 2	Year 3	Year 4	Year 5	
5	Sales	100,000	140,000	196,000	274,400	384,160	
6							
7	Production costs	60,000	84,000	117,600	164,640	230,496	
8	Fixed costs	50,000	52,500	55,125	57,881	60,775	
9							
10	Profit/Loss	- 10,000	3,500	23,275	51,879	92,889	
11							

Sheet1 / Sheet2 / Sheet3 /

Ready

Manipulating cells with formulas

If you insert or delete rows or columns, Excel will adjust the cell references in formulas – as far as it can. If you delete a cell that is referenced in a formula, you will have to rewrite the formula.

- ● Basic concepts
- ● Entering and formatting data
    - ○ Relative cell addresses
    - ○ Absolute and mixed cell addresses
- ● Basic formulas and functions
    - ○ Exploring different scenarios
- ● Editing and organising data
    - ○ **Moving cells with formulas**
    - ○ **Inserting cells into formulas**
- ● Charts
    - ○ **Deleting cells from formulas**
    - ○ **Summary - cells referenced by formulas**
- ○ Advanced formulas and functions
- ○ Importing objects into a workbook
    - ○ The IF function
- ○ Distributing your worksheets

Skill Builder **4.25**

1   Start a new worksheet and enter into it the data and formulas shown here.

	A	B	C	D
1		May	June	July
2	Hardware	12,340	17,690	13,575
3	Software	6,544	4,763	5,894
4	Consumables	523	639	254
5	Total sales	=SUM(B2:B4)	=SUM(C2:C4)	=SUM(D2:D4)
6				
7	Premises	350	350	350
8	Wages	2,400	2,400	2,400
9	Heat & Light		365	
10	Total costs	=SUM(B7:B9)	=SUM(C7:C9)	=SUM(D7:D9)
11				
12	Profit	=B5 - B10	=C5 - C10	=D5 - D10

2   Edit C7 so it contains the formula '=350 + 365', then delete row 9, 'Heat & Light'. What do the **Total costs** formulas now read?

3   Insert a new row above **Consumables**, entering this data.

| Services | 0 | 450 | 825 |

What do the **Total sales** formulas now read?

4   Insert a new row above **Premises**, entering this data.

| Purchases | 9,420 | 11,155 | 9,548 |

What do the **Total costs** formulas now read? Why haven't they changed?

> If you leave a blank row above the Totals row in a table and include its cells in your formulas, you can easily insert new rows above the blank.

The IF function

The IF function has this shape:
= IF(test, result-if-true, result-if-false)

Note that the parts are separated by commas, and that the 'result-if-true' and 'result-if-false' can be numbers, text or calculations.

In this example, we will use IF tests on students' marks to see if they've passed.

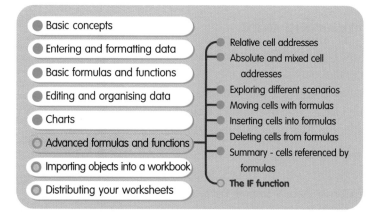

- Basic concepts
- Entering and formatting data
- Basic formulas and functions
- Editing and organising data
- Charts
- Advanced formulas and functions
- Importing objects into a workbook
- Distributing your worksheets

- Relative cell addresses
- Absolute and mixed cell addresses
- Exploring different scenarios
- Moving cells with formulas
- Inserting cells into formulas
- Deleting cells from formulas
- Summary - cells referenced by formulas
- **The IF function**

Skill Builder 4.26

1 Open the *students.xls* worksheet from the Resource Bank *Module 4* folder.

2 Write an IF function in C4 that will work like this:

If the mark in B4 is more than or equal to the pass mark in D1, the test should display 'Pass', otherwise it should display 'Fail'.

3 Copy the formula down to C16.

4 Compare the display with the marks. Do you see 'Pass' for those students with marks of 55 or more?

5 Save the file in your work folder.

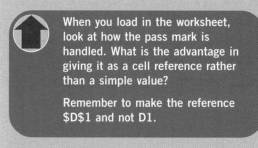

When you load in the worksheet, look at how the pass mark is handled. What is the advantage in giving it as a cell reference rather than a simple value?

Remember to make the reference D1 and not D1.

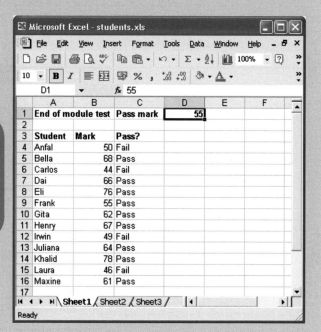

Importing objects into a workbook

Importing data

Text files can be opened by Excel. If they contain data organised into columns, either by spaces, tabs, commas or other delimiters, the **Text Import Wizard** will split the data into columns and rows.

You can import a text file into a worksheet with the **Data > Import External Data > Import Data...** command.

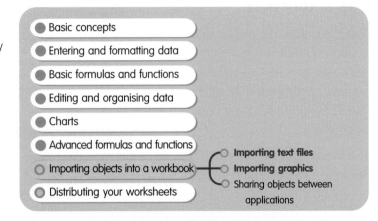

Skill Builder 4.27

1 Open the file *members.txt* from the Resource Bank *Module 4* folder. This list of club members has three fields: forename, surname and age, delimited by tabs. The **Text Import Wizard** should split the text into three columns.

2 Insert three rows at the top of the sheet.

3 In C1 type the heading: **Rackets Tennis Club**. Format it in bold, 14 point, and centre it across C1:E1

4 In A3 to C3 type the headings: **Forename, Surname, Age**.

5 Insert the picture file *rackets.bmp* from the *Module 4* folder. Reduce it down to about 4 rows high and place it at the top of the G column.

6 Save the file as *members.xls* in your work folder.

Your worksheet should look like this

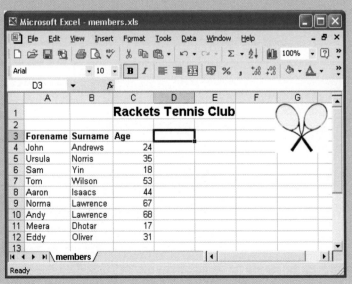

You can also paste images, text and data from other applications

Sharing objects between applications

Objects created in one application can be embedded in others in several ways. If they are linked, then the embedded copy of the object will change if the original is updated. Work through this Skill Builder and see for yourself.

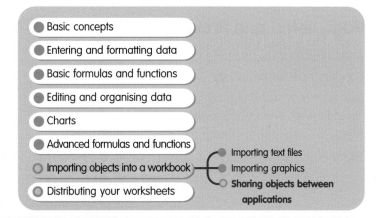

- Basic concepts
- Entering and formatting data
- Basic formulas and functions
- Editing and organising data
- Charts
- Advanced formulas and functions
- Importing objects into a workbook
  - Importing text files
  - Importing graphics
  - **Sharing objects between applications**
- Distributing your worksheets

Skill Builder **4.28**

1 Run Word and open the file *estimate.doc* from the Resource Bank *Module 4* folder. Move the insertion point to the line below the first paragraph.

2 Use the **Insert > Object...** command. At the **Insert** dialogue box, select the **Create from File** tab. Click the **Browse** button and locate *estimate.xls*. Tick the **Link to file** option and click **Insert** or **OK**.

Your worksheet should look like this

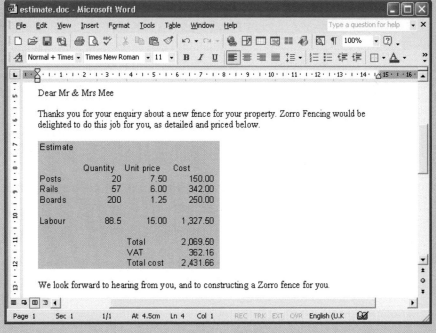

3 Switch back to Excel and open the file *estimate.xls* from the *Module 4* folder.

4 Change the number of posts to 21, and boards to 210.

5 Switch back to Word. Look at the estimate again. Has it changed?

Distributing your worksheets

Page setup and Preview

A worksheet can be printed by simply clicking the **Print** button 🖨 but the results may not be very readable! You should always preview the output, and adjust the page setup to get a better layout on the printed pages.

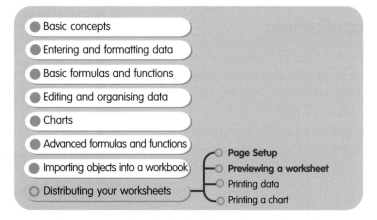

- Basic concepts
- Entering and formatting data
- Basic formulas and functions
- Editing and organising data
- Charts
- Advanced formulas and functions
- Importing objects into a workbook
- Distributing your worksheets
  - Page Setup
  - Previewing a worksheet
  - Printing data
  - Printing a chart

Skill Builder **4.29**

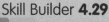

1 Open the *results.xls* workbook in the Resource Bank *Module 4* folder.

2 Use the **Page Setup** dialogue box to specify that rows 4 and 5 and column A are repeated on every page.

3 Check that the **Paper size** is correct for your printer.

4 Go to **Print Preview** and look through the page to see how the data fits. If some pages contain only one or two rows or columns of data, use a **Scaling** option in the **Page Setup** dialogue box to fit the data on more economically.

5 Set the **Orientation** to landscape and return to the **Print Preview** to see the effect. Change the orientation back to portrait if that gives a better printout.

6 Increase the **Left margin** by 1 cm to give more room for stapling.

7 Centre the printout horizontally, but not vertically.

8 Add the header 'Summary results: Year 1' on the left of every sheet, and use the standard footer to display 'Page 1 of ?'.

9 Close the **Page Setup** dialogue box and close the **Print Preview**.

10 Save the file in your work folder.

Printing

For a single copy of the occupied part of a sheet, just click 🖨.

If you want several copies, or you only want to print part of the sheet, you must go into the **Print** dialogue box which gives you more control of the printout.

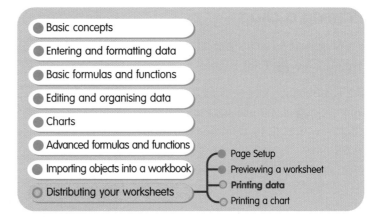

- Basic concepts
- Entering and formatting data
- Basic formulas and functions
- Editing and organising data
- Charts
- Advanced formulas and functions
- Importing objects into a workbook
- Distributing your worksheets
  - Page Setup
  - Previewing a worksheet
  - **Printing data**
  - Printing a chart

Skill Builder **4.30**

1 Open your copy of *results.xls* workbook, saved in Skill Builder 4.29.

2 Use **Print Preview** to check that the printout is as you want it.

3 Open the **Print** dialogue box.

4 Set the options to print 2 copies of the first two pages.

5 Start the printout, then close the worksheet.

To print only a part a sheet, select it first before starting the Print routine then use the **Selection** option

Turn on **Collate** if you are printing multiple copies of multiple page sheets

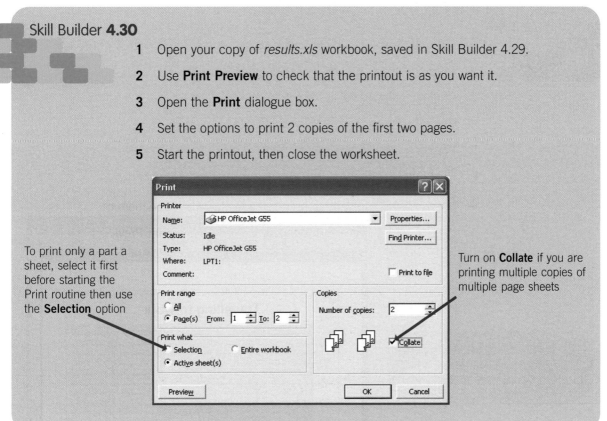

Printing a chart

If a chart is in its own sheet, to print it, just click the 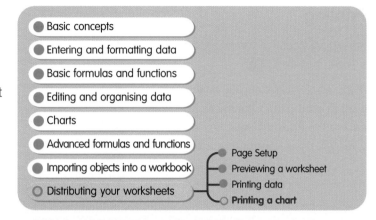 **Print** button.

If it is embedded in a worksheet, select it and click 🖨 if you just want to print the chart. Deselect it, by clicking elsewhere in the sheet, if you want to print the chart as part of the larger sheet.

- ● Basic concepts
- ● Entering and formatting data
- ● Basic formulas and functions
- ● Editing and organising data
- ● Charts
- ● Advanced formulas and functions
- ● Importing objects into a workbook
- ○ Distributing your worksheets
  - ● Page Setup
  - ● Previewing a worksheet
  - ● Printing data
  - ○ **Printing a chart**

Skill Builder **4.31**

1 Open the *travel.xls* workbook that you saved in Skill Builder 4.21.

2 Go to the sheet containing the line graph.

3 Print one copy of the line graph.

4 Go to the sheet containing the embedded bar chart.

5 Print one copy of the chart by itself.

6 Print one copy of the sheet, showing the data and the chart.

7 Close the workbook.

> ⬆ If you want to know how a sheet will look when printed, use **Print Preview** on the **File** menu.

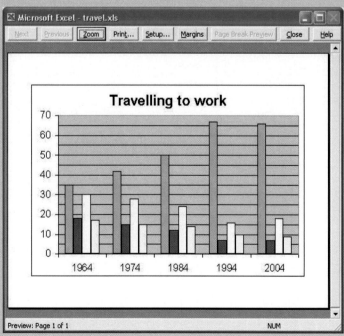

Now try Assignment 4.3

Module 5

DATABASES

A database is a set of files containing data and others which have the tools that are used to get information out of the raw data. Microsoft Access is the leading database management software. As well as data entry and editing facilities, it offers:

- wizards for creating forms, reports and queries
- easy-to-use but very effective methods for sorting and searching through data
- full control over the layout and appearance of forms and reports, on screen and paper.

○ Using the computer and managing files

○ Word processing

● Spreadsheets

○ Databases

○ Presentations

○ Information and communication

 Throughout this unit you will be asked to open files that are supplied in the Resource Bank. They can be found on the Resource Bank CD or in the folder which your tutor may have set up for use with this course.

Getting started

What is a database?

A database is an organised set of data along with the tools that are used to get information out of it. It may be simple, e.g. a list of names and addresses, with a means of producing mailing labels; or very complex, e.g. one for a school could hold details of the pupils, staff and the lessons, and be capable of producing class lists, timetables and the details of any individual person.

- Getting started
- Setting up a database
- Working with tables
- Working with forms
- Sorting records in a database
- Working with queries
- Relational databases
- Creating reports and printing

- **What is a database?**
- **Before you begin**
- Launching Microsoft Access
- The Microsoft Access work area
- Menu and toolbar basics
- Using application Help
- Closing Microsoft Access

Database managemement system

To handle a database, you need a *database management system*. The one we will be using is Access, part of the Microsoft Office suite.

Data is stored in tables, organised by rows and columns. A database may have several tables, with each holding a distinct set of data. One for a business might have a Supplier table, a Client table, an Employee table and a Stock table.

Each row contains a *record*, which holds the data for one member of the table, e.g. in a client database there would be a record for each client.

The smallest item of data is a *field*. In that client database, there would be a field for the surname, one for forenames, another for the telephone number, several for the different parts of the address, and perhaps many others.

As well as tables, a database may contain objects for managing the data. The main ones are:

Forms – used to enter, edit or display data one record at a time. This is often better that working directly with the tables.

Queries – used to select records, e.g. clients with overdue debts, or the students in class 3B. The query may contain the full details of each matching record, or just selected fields. The data selected by a query is called a *dynaset*.

Reports – used to print information from a table or query, and may include summaries of the information in selected fields.

In an Access database, the tables, queries and reports are all stored in a single file.

Field name   Fields

Company Name	Contact	Street	Town	Telephone	Credit limit
Brown's	John Brown	24 Market Square	Newtown	010 123 6543	£250.00
Fresh 'n' Fruity	Mrs Pears	12 High Street	Newtown	010 123 4567	£500.00
Reggie's Vegs	Reg	187 High Street	Newtown	010 123 4789	£0.00

Records

The Access work area

Microsoft Access is a typical Windows application, with menus, toolbars, and windows, but with one noticeable difference. When you open a database, you are not taken directly into a document, as in Word. At first, you only see the Database window. Tables, forms, and other objects are opened from here as they are needed.

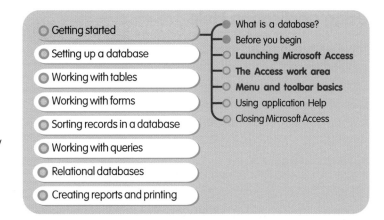

- Getting started
  - What is a database?
  - Before you begin
  - **Launching Microsoft Access**
  - **The Access work area**
  - **Menu and toolbar basics**
  - Using application Help
  - Closing Microsoft Access
- Setting up a database
- Working with tables
- Working with forms
- Sorting records in a database
- Working with queries
- Relational databases
- Creating reports and printing

Skill Builder 5.1

1 Run Access, either from the **Start** menu or its desktop icon.

2 In the **Microsoft Access** dialogue box, select **More files** in the **Open an existing file** section.

3 Open the file *clients.mdb* from the Resource Bank *Module 5* folder.

4 In the **Database** window, double-click on the *Client list* to open the table.

5 Explore the menus to see the range of commands available.

Menu bar

Standard toolbar

Database window

Object bar – click a type to display its existing objects and Create tools

Table window

Field names

Record

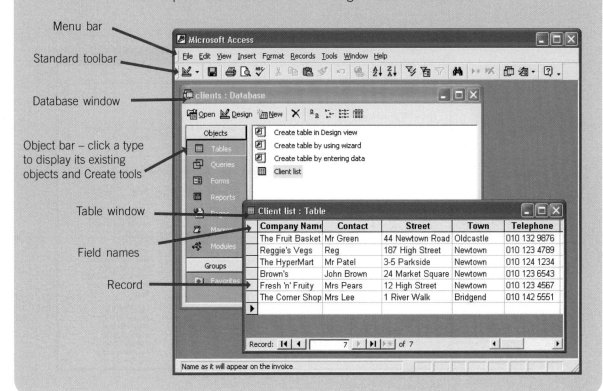

Using application Help

There's lots of help available in Access – the tricky part is finding the precise information that you need. Try to be as specific as possible when using the Assistant or the Answer Wizard.

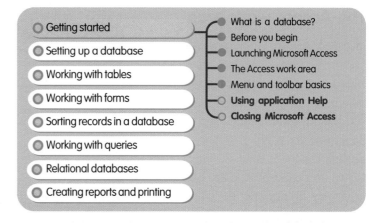

Skill Builder **5.2**

1   Use the **Help > Microsoft Access Help** command to open the Help system.

2   On the **Contents** tab, look in the *Getting Help* folder and find out how to print a Help page.

3   Use the Answer Wizard to find out about the types of data that Access can store – try 'datatype' as a keyword.

4   Close the Help system.

5   Close down Access.

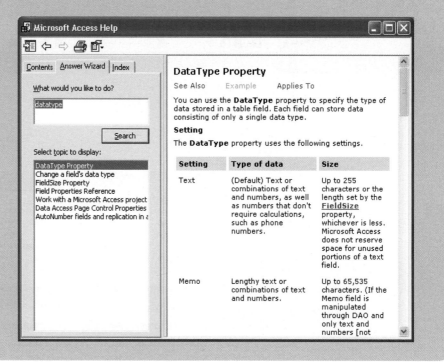

Setting up a database

Creating a new table

Over the course of this module, we will create and use a stock database that holds details of products and their suppliers. We will start by creating the database and the first table.

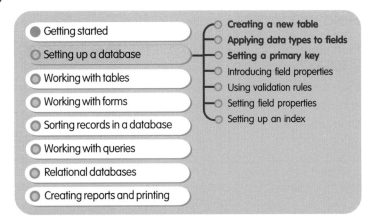

- ● Getting started
- ◐ Setting up a database
  - ○ **Creating a new table**
  - ○ **Applying data types to fields**
  - ○ **Setting a primary key**
  - ○ Introducing field properties
  - ○ Using validation rules
  - ○ Setting field properties
  - ○ Setting up an index
- ◐ Working with tables
- ◐ Working with forms
- ◐ Sorting records in a database
- ◐ Working with queries
- ◐ Relational databases
- ◐ Creating reports and printing

Skill Builder **5.3**

1 Use **File > New** to create a database. Save it as *stock.mdb*.

2 Create a new table in **Design** view, using the design given below. For each field, enter the name, select the data type, then type in the description.

Field name	Data type	Description
Product ID	AutoNumber	
Item	Text	Name and specification
Unit cost	Currency	Cost per item when last ordered
No in stock	Number	
Min quantity	Number	Reorder when stock gets this low
Last order	Date/Time	Date of last order
Supplier	Text	5-letter code for supplier

3 Select the *Product ID* field and click 🔑 to make it the primary key.

4 Save the table as *Products* and close it.

Your table design should look like this after the fields have been created and the primary key set

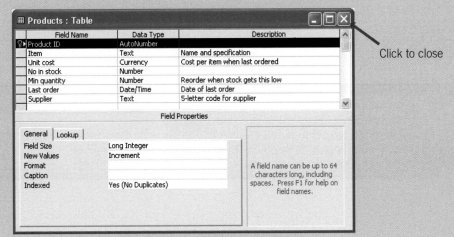

Click to close

Field properties

Field properties are best set before data is entered into the table. You can set them later, but data may be lost if a field size is reduced or its number type changed.

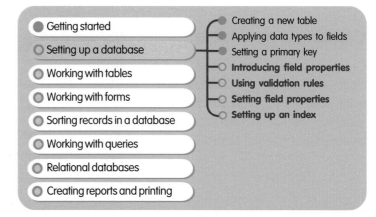

- Getting started
- Setting up a database
- Working with tables
- Working with forms
- Sorting records in a database
- Working with queries
- Relational databases
- Creating reports and printing

- Creating a new table
- Applying data types to fields
- Setting a primary key
- **Introducing field properties**
- **Using validation rules**
- **Setting field properties**
- **Setting up an index**

Skill Builder 5.4

1 Open your *stock.mdb* database, if it is not already open.

2 At the **Database** window, select the *Products* table and click ▨ Design the **Design** button to open the table in **Design** view.

3 Make the following changes to field properties.

Field name	Property	New value
Item	Field size	30
Unit cost	Format	Standard
No in stock	Field size	Integer
Min quantity	Field size	Integer
Min quantity	Validation rule	>=0 And <=100
Min quantity	Validation text	Enter a value between 0 and 100
Last order	Format	Short date
Supplier	Field size	5

4 Set indexes on the *Item* and *Last order* fields.

5 Save the changes and close the table.

If you close the table in **Design** view without saving, Access will ask you if you want to save the changes. Click **Yes** – unless you want to abandon the changes and leave the design as it was before.

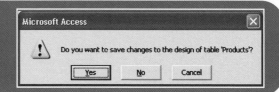

Working with tables

Adding data to a table

It is important that the data in a database is as accurate as possible, but don't worry too much when working through the next Skill Builder. Any errors can be corrected later after you have learnt about editing data.

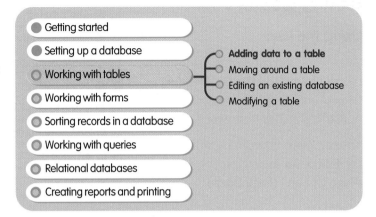

- ● Getting started
- ● Setting up a database
- ○ Working with tables
  - ○ **Adding data to a table**
  - ○ Moving around a table
  - ○ Editing an existing database
  - ○ Modifying a table
- ○ Working with forms
- ○ Sorting records in a database
- ○ Working with queries
- ○ Relational databases
- ○ Creating reports and printing

Skill Builder 5.5

1 Open the *stock.mdb* database that you saved in Skill Builder 5.4.

2 In the **Database** window, select the *Products* table and click 📇 Open the **Open** button to open the table in **Datasheet** view.

3 Enter the following data. Remember that the Product ID is an AutoNumber.

Product ID	Item	Unit cost	No in stock	Min quantity	Last order	Supplier
1	Pasta tongs, steel	1.25	24	10	12/03/2005	HKMAN
2	Whisk, balloon	2.70	12	5	04/12/2004	DUPON
3	Whisk,medium	2.15	29	20	04/12/2004	DUPON
4	Whisk, egg	1.55	19	10	04/12/2004	DUPON
5	Jar opener,V-grip	0.95	44	10	05/01/2005	HKMAN
6	Jar opener, strap	1.24	37	10	05/05/2005	CHDOM
7	Garlic press	3.47	48	20	16/04/2005	INTIM
8	Lemon juicer, steel tripod	6.75	14	10	24/02/2005	HKMAN
9	Lemon juicer, glass	1.15	12	20	09/02/2005	INTIM
10	Chef's tool set	19.95	15	10	11/02/2005	SHEFF

4 The data is saved automatically. Close the table when you have finished.

At first, all columns are the same width. You may prefer to make the Item column wider so that you can see the whole of the entries. Drag on the divider to the right of the field name at the top of the column to adjust the width, or double-click on it to get Access to adjust it for you. You will be prompted to save the layout changes when you close the table. There's more about setting column widths in the 'Modifying a table' lesson of the Electric Paper course.

Moving around a table

Using the keys

You can move from field to field within a record using **[Tab]**, **[Enter]**, **[←]**, **[→]**, **[Home]** and **[End]**. perhaps with **[Shift]** or **[Ctrl]** to modify their effects.

You can move between records using the **Edit > Go To** options, **[↑]**, **[↓]**, **[Page Up]** and **[Page Down]**.

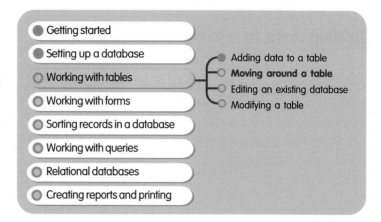

- Getting started
- Setting up a database
- Working with tables
  - Adding data to a table
  - **Moving around a table**
  - Editing an existing database
  - Modifying a table
- Working with forms
- Sorting records in a database
- Working with queries
- Relational databases
- Creating reports and printing

Movement keys

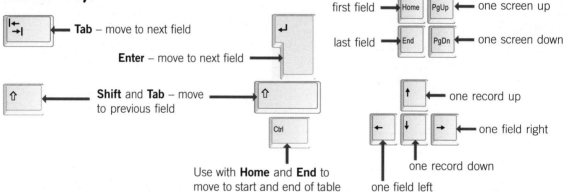

Tab – move to next field

Enter – move to next field

Shift and **Tab** – move to previous field

Use with **Home** and **End** to move to start and end of table

first field → Home

last field → End

PgUp → one screen up

PgDn → one screen down

↑ → one record up

→ → one field right

one record down

one field left

Using the navigation buttons

In a large database, the most efficient way to move around is with the navigation buttons in the lower-left of the window.

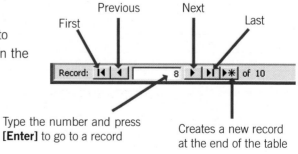

First
Previous
Next
Last

Record: |◀ ◀ | 8 | ▶ ▶| ▶* | of 10

Type the number and press **[Enter]** to go to a record

Creates a new record at the end of the table

 And don't forget that you can click into any visible field, and use the scroll bars to bring different areas of the table into view.

Editing an existing database

Data can be edited, to correct mistakes or update entries. The text and figures can be changed, deleted or added to as in any other Windows application.

To edit the text in a field, click into it or move to the cell and press **[F2]** to switch to edit mode.

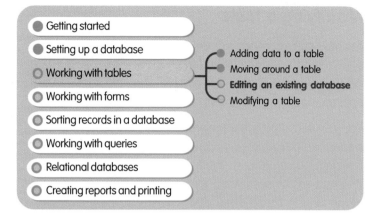

- Getting started
- Setting up a database
- Working with tables
  - Adding data to a table
  - Moving around a table
  - **Editing an existing database**
  - Modifying a table
- Working with forms
- Sorting records in a database
- Working with queries
- Relational databases
- Creating reports and printing

Skill Builder 5.6

1 Open your *stock.mdb* database, saved in Skill Builder 5.5.

2 In the **Database** window, select the *Products* table and click ⊞ Open the **Open** button to open the table in **Datasheet** view.

3 Compare your records with the data given on page 99. If there are any erorrs, correct them now.

4 Make the following changes:

The shop has sold 2 pasta tongs, 3 balloon whisks and 1 chef's tool set. 50 glass lemon juicers have arrived from International Imports (INTIM). Clear its *Last order* field and update all the *No in stock* values.

The egg whisk supplier should be China Domestic Goods (CHDOM), and the last order was placed on Jan 15th 2005.

The garlic press *Unit cost* should be 3.74.

5 Close the table when you have finished.

The table should look like this after editing

	Product ID	Item	Unit cost	No in stock	Min quantity	Last order	Supplier
	1	Pasta tongs, steel	1.25	22	10	12/03/2005	HKMAN
	2	Whisk, balloon	2.70	9	5	04/12/2004	DUPON
	3	Whisk, medium	2.15	29	20	04/12/2004	DUPON
	4	Whisk, egg	1.55	19	10	15/01/2005	CHDOM
	5	Jar opener, V-grip	0.95	44	10	05/01/2005	HKMAN
	6	Jar opener, strap	1.24	37	10	05/05/2005	CHDOM
▶	7	Garlic press	3.74	48	20	16/04/2005	INTIM
	8	Lemon juicer, steel tripod	6.75	14	10	24/02/2005	HKMAN
	9	Lemon juicer, glass	1.15	62	20		INTIM
	10	Chef's tool set	19.95	14	10	11/02/2005	SHEFF
*	(AutoNumber)		0.00	0	0		

⊞ Products : Table

Record: ◀◀ ◀ 7 ▶ ▶◀ ▶* of 10

Modifying a table

Records can be inserted or deleted from a table, and fields can be added or deleted – but remember that once deleted, data cannot be restored.

You can also modify the appearance of a table, adjusting column widths or freezing key columns on the left so that they can still be seen when the far right of the table is scrolled into view.

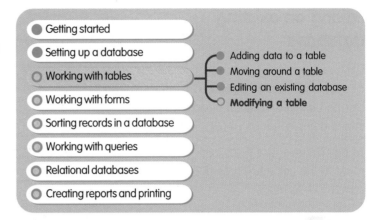

- Getting started
- Setting up a database
  - Adding data to a table
  - Moving around a table
  - Editing an existing database
  - **Modifying a table**
- Working with tables
- Working with forms
- Sorting records in a database
- Working with queries
- Relational databases
- Creating reports and printing

Skill Builder 5.7

1 Open the *stock.mdb* database, saved in Skill Builder 5.6, then open the *Products* table in **Datasheet** view.

2 Insert these records:

Product ID	Item	Unit cost	No in stock	Min quantity	Last order	Supplier
11	Meat mallet, steel	9.95	0	10	06/05/2005	HKMAN
12	Kitchen shears	14.49	0	5	06/05/2005	HKMAN

3 Click ⚒ ▾, the **View** button, to go to **Design** view.

4 Insert two new fields:

Field name	Data type	Description
Order quantity	Integer	Minimum order quantity
Last Delivery	Date/Time	Date of last delivery

5 Select the *Supplier* field and drag it down so that it is the last in the list.

6 Save the changes and click ⚒ ▾, the **View** button, to go to **Datasheet** view.

7 Freeze the first two columns.

8 Enter the *Order quantity* and *Last delivery* data as shown below.

9 Close the table.

Product ID	Item	Min quantity	Last order	Order quantity	Last delivery	Supplier
1	Pasta tongs, steel	10	12/03/2005	20		HKMAN
2	Whisk, balloon	5	04/12/2004	10		DUPON
3	Whisk, medium	20	04/12/2004	25		DUPON
4	Whisk, egg	10	15/01/2005	25		CHDOM
5	Jar opener, V-grip	10	05/01/2005	10		HKMAN
6	Jar opener, strap	10	05/05/2005	10		CHDOM
7	Garlic press	20	16/04/2005	50		INTIM
8	Lemon juicer, steel tripod	10	24/02/2005	5		HKMAN
9	Lemon juicer, glass	20		50	05/05/2005	INTIM
10	Chef's tool set	10	11/02/2005	25		SHEFF
11	Meat mallet, steel	10	06/05/2005	5		HKMAN
12	Kitchen shears	5	06/05/2005	5		HKMAN

Working with forms

Forms and the Form Wizard

Tables provide a compact way to display data, but they are not user-friendly. A form is an alternative way to view data, displaying the data from one record at a time. It is normally easier to enter, edit and read data on a form than in a table.

The simplest way to create a form is with the **Form Wizard**.

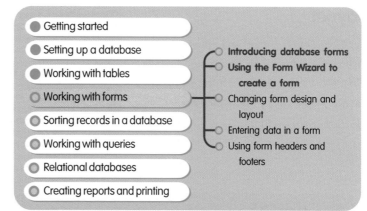

- Getting started
- Setting up a database
- Working with tables
- Working with forms
- Sorting records in a database
- Working with queries
- Relational databases
- Creating reports and printing

  - **Introducing database forms**
  - **Using the Form Wizard to create a form**
  - Changing form design and layout
  - Entering data in a form
  - Using form headers and footers

Skill Builder **5.8**

1   Open the *stock.mdb* database from Skill Builder 5.7.

2   In the **Database** window select *Forms* in the **Objects** bar.

3   Select **Create form by using wizard**.

4   Check that the *Products* table is selected in the **Tables/Queries** list – there shouldn't be any alternative at this stage. (See the Tip below.)

5   Click >> to add all the fields to the **Selected Fields** list then click **Next**.

6   Choose the **Columnar** layout then click **Next**.

7   Choose any style then click **Next.**

8   Give the form a title.

9   Select the option to open the form to view the data and click **Finish**.

Your form should have this layout, though its style may be different

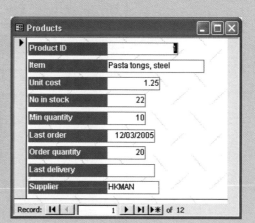

At the first stage of the Wizard there is a Tables/Queries list. In a relational database (see page 108), there will be several tables to choose from. If you have saved queries (see page 113), you could create a form based on the subset produced by a query.

Changing form design and layout

The layout, size, font and colours of fields and labels can be changed easily. The techniques are much the same as in the other Office applications.

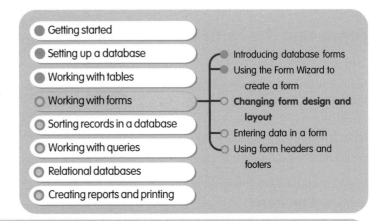

- Getting started
- Setting up a database
- Working with tables
- Working with forms
- Sorting records in a database
- Working with queries
- Relational databases
- Creating reports and printing

- Introducing database forms
- Using the Form Wizard to create a form
- **Changing form design and layout**
- Entering data in a form
- Using form headers and footers

Skill Builder 5.9

1   Open your *stock.mdb* database and open the *Products* form.

2   Click 🖉 ▾ to switch to **Design** view.

3   Set all the text boxes and labels in Times New Roman, 11 point. Use the **Format > Size > To Fit** command to adjust the boxes for the larger type.

4   Format the labels in bold.

5   Make the number and date text boxes the same size, and right align them.

6   Click 🖫 to save your changes, then click 🖽 ▾ to go to **Form** view.

> If you change the layout or sizes, don't forget about the options on the **Format** menu.

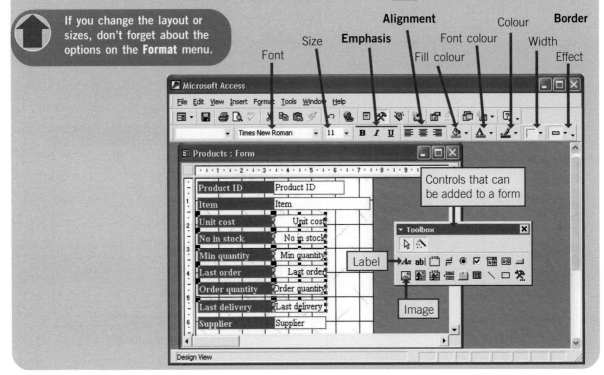

Entering data in a form

Data can be entered and edited in a form just as it can in a table.

Use the mouse or the **[Tab]** and arrow keys to move between fields.

Use the navigation bar to move between records.

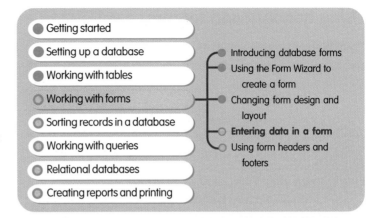

- Getting started
- Setting up a database
- Working with tables
- Working with forms
- Sorting records in a database
- Working with queries
- Relational databases
- Creating reports and printing

  - Introducing database forms
  - Using the Form Wizard to create a form
  - Changing form design and layout
  - **Entering data in a form**
  - Using form headers and footers

Skill Builder **5.10**

1 Open your *stock.mdb* database then open the *Products* form.

2 20 steel meat mallets have been delivered. Go to the record (no 11), update the *No in stock* and enter today's date in the *Last Delivery* field.

3 The V-grip jar opener is to be discontinued. Delete its record (no 5).

4 Insert these records:

Product ID	Item	Unit cost	No in stock	Min qty	Last order	Order qty	Last delivery	Supplier
13	Meat mallet, pine	7.40	0	5	06/05/2005	5		IDEAL
14	Rolling pin, pine	4.49	0	10	06/05/2005	10		IDEAL
15	Chopping block	8.95	0	5	06/05/2005	10		IDEAL

5 Change the *Unit cost* of the pasta tongs (record 1) to 1.30.

6 Close the *Products* form and open the *Products* table. Check that your changes and new records are visible there. Close the table.

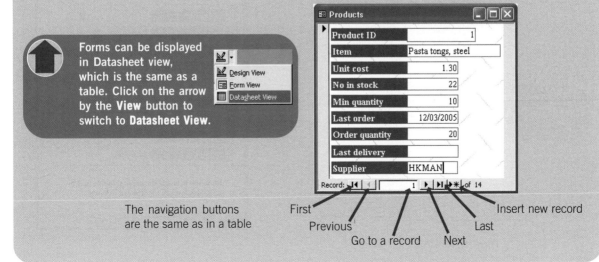

Forms can be displayed in Datasheet view, which is the same as a table. Click on the arrow by the **View** button to switch to **Datasheet View**.

Design View
Form View
Datasheet View

Products

Product ID	1
Item	Pasta tongs, steel
Unit cost	1.30
No in stock	22
Min quantity	10
Last order	12/03/2005
Order quantity	20
Last delivery	
Supplier	HKMAN

Record: ◄◄ ◄ 1 ► ►I ►* of 14

The navigation buttons are the same as in a table

First
Previous
Go to a record
Next
Last
Insert new record

Using headers and footers

Form headers and footers can be just
decorative, or used to carry reminders
for people entering data.

 If Form Headers/Footers were
turned on for you when the form
was created, they will have been
minimised. Turn them off and on
again to open them up properly.

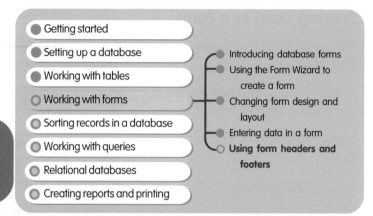

- Getting started
- Setting up a database
- Working with tables
- Working with forms
  - Introducing database forms
  - Using the Form Wizard to create a form
  - Changing form design and layout
  - Entering data in a form
  - **Using form headers and footers**
- Sorting records in a database
- Working with queries
- Relational databases
- Creating reports and printing

Skill Builder 5.11

1 Open your *stock.mdb* database and open the *Products* form.

2 Click 📉 ▾ to switch to **Design** view.

3 Turn on the **Form Headers/Footers**.

4 Click **Aa** and add a **Label** control to the header. Type in 'Cook's Supplies'.
Click on the background when you have done it, then click the label to
select it. Format the text in Arial, 14 point bold.

5 Add a Label to the footer, with the text 'Remember to add the order quantity
to the no in stock when recording a delivery'. Set its background to trans-
parent and font colour to black.

6 Click 💾 to save your changes,
then click 📧 ▾ to go to Form view.

With the header and footer text in place,
your form should look something like this.

 A control is an object on a form.
Labels and fields are the two
controls most often used.

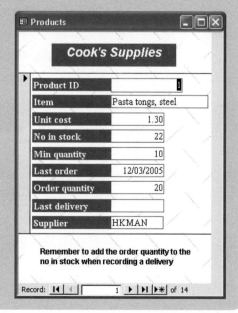

 Now try Assignment 5.1

106

Sorting records in a database

Sorting records in a table

Records are normally displayed in the order in which they were entered, or in the order of the primary key, if set. They can be quickly sorted into order on any field (or set of fields) using the **Sort** buttons. The sort can be $\frac{A}{Z}\downarrow$ ascending or $\frac{Z}{A}\downarrow$ descending, and will be in alphabetic, numeric or date order, depending upon the values in the field.

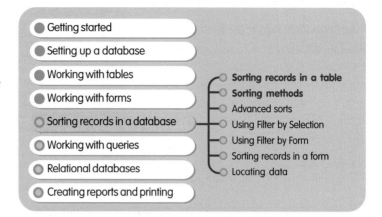

- Getting started
- Setting up a database
- Working with tables
- Working with forms
- Sorting records in a database
- Working with queries
- Relational databases
- Creating reports and printing

- **Sorting records in a table**
- **Sorting methods**
- Advanced sorts
- Using Filter by Selection
- Using Filter by Form
- Sorting records in a form
- Locating data

Skill Builder 5.12

1 Copy *cars.mdb* from the Resource Bank *Module 5* folder to your work folder, then open your copy of the database.

2 Open the *Used cars* table.

3 Sort the table by ascending order of *Make* then *Model* .

4 Restore the original order.

5 Sort the table into ascending order of *Year*. How old is the oldest car?

6 Sort the table so that the highest mileage car is at the top.

7 Sort the table in descending order of *Price* then *Type*. What's the first thing you that you need to do?

8 How would you sort the table to produce the order shown below?

Used cars : Table

ID	Make	Model	Engine	Year	Mileage	Type	Price
41	Nissan	Micra	1.2	2004	3,000	Hatchback	6,499
8	Ford	Escort	1.3	1992	66,000	Estate	799
45	Austin	Mini Cooper	1.3	1992	70,000	Saloon	4,395
42	Nissan	Micra	1.3	1997	67,000	Hatchback	2,989
13	Ford	Ka	1.3	1997	88,000	Hatchback	2,295
34	Toyota	Yaris	1.3	2001	11,000	Hatchback	6,995
4	Ford	Ka	1.3	2001	27,000	Hatchback	3,999
3	Ford	Fiesta	1.3	2001	40,000	Hatchback	3,499
33	Toyota	Yaris	1.3	2002	13,000	Hatchback	7,495
12	Ford	Ka	1.3	2004	16,000	Hatchback	4,599
30	Toyota	Corolla	1.4	2001	30,000	Hatchback	5,795
20	Citroen	C3	1.4	2002	2,500	Hatchback	8,195
24	Citroen	Xsara	1.4	2003	76,000	Estate	5,995
37	Nissan	Almera	1.5	2000	61,000	Hatchback	3,995

Record: ◄◄ ◄ 1 ► ►I ►* of 44

> Sorting on a column will bring together those records with the same value in that field, e.g. those in the same town. They can then be selected as a group.

Advanced sorts

The Advanced Filter/Sort facility is highly flexible, allowing you to sort on any number of fields, and in either order on each field. The sort can be saved as a query for later reuse.

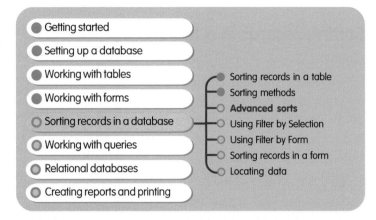

Skill Builder 5.13

1 Open your copy of the *cars.mdb* database, saved in Skill Builder 5.12.

2 Open the *Used cars* table.

3 Use the Advanced Filter/Sort to sort the table by ascending order of *Make* and *Model* then by descending order of *Price*.

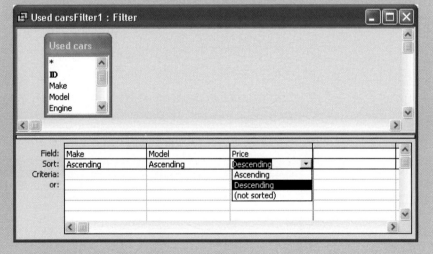

Setting the sort order in the Advanced Filter/Sort window

4 Save the query with the name *Model and Price*.

5 Close the filter window and close the *Used cars* table.

6 At the Database window, select *Queries* on the **Objects** bar.

7 Double-click on *Model and Price* to open it. What do you see?

8 Close the table and the database.

Using Filter by Selection

Filter by Selection is easy to use, but it only allows you to filter on one criterion at a time. However, as you can filter the results of an earlier filter – as many times as you like – the method can produce a very specific subset.

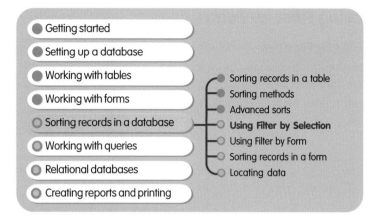

- Getting started
- Setting up a database
- Working with tables
  - Sorting records in a table
  - Sorting methods
  - Advanced sorts
- Working with forms
- Sorting records in a database
  - **Using Filter by Selection**
  - Using Filter by Form
  - Sorting records in a form
  - Locating data
- Working with queries
- Relational databases
- Creating reports and printing

Skill Builder 5.14

1 Open your *cars.mdb* database, saved in Skill Builder 5.13.

2 Open the *Used cars* table.

3 Use **Filter by Selection** to find hatchbacks from the year 2000.

4 Use **Filter by Selection** to find estates from the year 2000 or later, with an engine size of 1.4.

5 How would you filter the table to get these results?

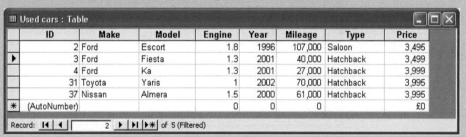

	ID	Make	Model	Engine	Year	Mileage	Type	Price
	2	Ford	Escort	1.8	1996	107,000	Saloon	3,495
▶	3	Ford	Fiesta	1.3	2001	40,000	Hatchback	3,499
	4	Ford	Ka	1.3	2001	27,000	Hatchback	3,999
	31	Toyota	Yaris	1	2002	70,000	Hatchback	3,995
	37	Nissan	Almera	1.5	2000	61,000	Hatchback	3,995
✳	(AutoNumber)			0	0	0		£0

Record: |◀ ◀ | 2 | ▶ |▶| |▶✳| of 5 (Filtered)

6 Use **Filter by Selection** to find saloons with an engine size of 1.8.

7 Go to the **Advanced Filter/Sort** window and save the query as 'Saloons 1800'.

8 Close the table and the database.

> If you had tried to save the query as 'Saloons 1.8', you would have had an error message as a name cannot contain a '.' dot.

Using Filter by Form

Filter by Form lets you set criteria in several fields at once, and it also has the very useful **Or** option which allows you to look for different values in the same field.

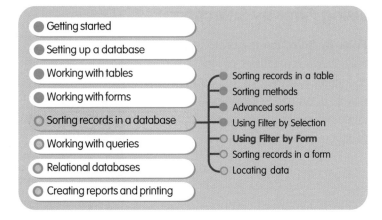

- Getting started
- Setting up a database
- Working with tables
  - Sorting records in a table
  - Sorting methods
  - Advanced sorts
- Working with forms
- Sorting records in a database
  - Using Filter by Selection
  - **Using Filter by Form**
  - Sorting records in a form
- Working with queries
- Relational databases
  - Locating data
- Creating reports and printing

Skill Builder **5.15**

1 Open your *cars.mdb* database.

2 Open the *Used cars* table.

3 Use **Filter by Form** to find saloons or hatchbacks with engines of 1.3.

4 Use **Filter by Form** to find any Citroen or Nissan hatchbacks.

5 What filter would you have to create to get these results?

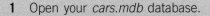

	ID	Make	Model	Engine	Year	Mileage	Type	Price
▶	10 Ford		Fiesta	1.6	2000	68,000	Hatchback	4,295
	6 Ford		Cougar	2.5	2000	100,000	Hatchback	4,499
	14 Ford		Mondeo	2	2001	70,000	Hatchback	6,499
	7 Ford		Cougar	2.5	2001	31,000	Hatchback	8,995
	4 Ford		Ka	1.3	2001	27,000	Hatchback	3,999
	3 Ford		Fiesta	1.3	2001	40,000	Hatchback	3,499
*	(AutoNumber)			0	0	0		0

Record: 1 of 6 (Filtered)

6 Use **Filter by Form** to find cars with an engine size of 1.3 or 1.4, from 2001 or 2002. You will need to use three **Or** tabs.

7 Save the last query as 'Mid-size 2001/02'.

8 Close the table and the database.

Remember that the subsets produced by filters can be filtered and sorted just like full tables.

Sorting records in a form

This is basically the same as sorting in a table – you select the field you want to sort on then click the 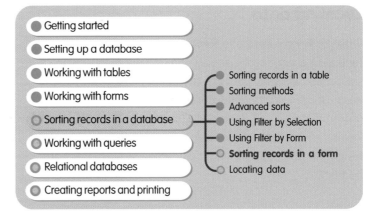 ascending or descending toolbar button. The only real difference is that you can only sort on a single field.

Skill Builder 5.16

1 Open your *cars.mdb* database.

2 Open the *All cars* form.

3 Sort the table by descending order of *Year* – you should find that a Ford Mondeo comes to the top.

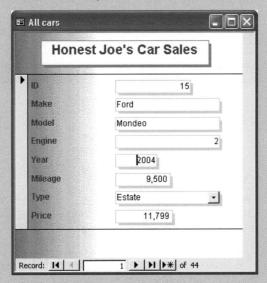

4 Restore the original order.

5 Sort the table into ascending order of *Price*. What is the cheapest car?

6 Sort the table so that the highest mileage car is at the top.

Locating data

When running a **Find** or a **Replace** routine in a large table, specify the search as tightly as possible. If you know which field the data is in, look only in that field – it is much faster than looking in the entire table. Selecting which part of a field to match can also be helpful.

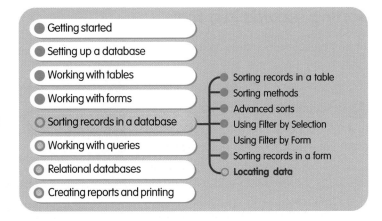

- Getting started
- Setting up a database
- Working with tables
  - Sorting records in a table
  - Sorting methods
  - Advanced sorts
- Working with forms
- Sorting records in a database
  - Using Filter by Selection
  - Using Filter by Form
  - Sorting records in a form
- Working with queries
- Relational databases
  - **Locating data**
- Creating reports and printing

Skill Builder **5.17**

1 Open your *cars.mdb* database.

2 Open the *Used cars* table.

3 Use the **Find** routine to search for a car with 'Sports' in the *Type* field. How many are there?

4 Look for a Mini and a Mini Cooper. If you set up a **Find** like this, it should locate both models.

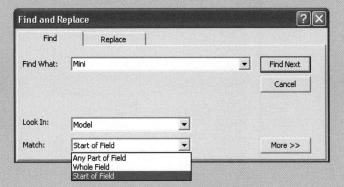

5 The Ford Cougars are coupes not hatchbacks. Use **Replace** on the Type field to change the entries. You must use the **Replace** button to change one at a time, and only after checking that the entry is in a Cougar record.

> When doing a selective replace, move the **Find and Replace** dialogue box out of the way so that you can see the records more clearly.

Working with queries

Creating a query and using criteria

There are two parts to creating a query:

❖ Selecting the *fields* to be shown in the query. You may not need all the fields, for example you would only want names and addressses for a mailshot.

❖ Selecting the *records* to include.

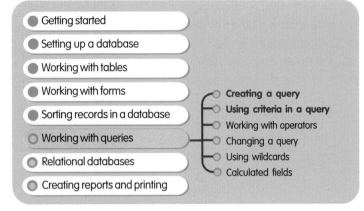

The **Simple Query Wizard** can be used to select fields from a table. It does not select records, but a query started here can be modified in the **Query Design** window. The following query will select saloons from the *Used cars* table.

Skill Builder 5.18

1 Open your *cars.mdb* database.

2 In the Database window select *Queries* in the **Objects** bar.

3 Use the wizard to set up a query based on the *Used cars* table to display the *Make*, *Model*, *Engine*, *Year* and *Price* fields. Call it 'Saloons'.

4 Take the query into **Design** view.

5 Add the Type field by selecting it from the field list of the first blank column. Do not tick its Show box.

6 In the Criteria row for *Type*, enter 'Saloon'.

7 Click **!** , the **Run** button.

The resulting query should look like this

Make	Model	Engine	Year	Price
Ford	Escort	1.8	1996	3,495
Ford	Mondeo	1.8	1994	650
Citroen	C3	1.4	2002	8,195
Citroen	C3	1.6	2003	7,495
Citroen	Xsara	1.8	1998	2,495
Austin	Mini	1	1989	995
Austin	Mini Cooper	1.3	1992	4,395
*		0	0	0

Saloons : Select Query

Record: 1 of 7

Working with operators

Entering a value as the criterion will only find exact matches. To find those that fall in a range, e.g. cars below a certain price, you must use the *operators*:

>	greater than
<	less than
<>	not equal to
>=	greater than or equal to
<=	less than or equal to

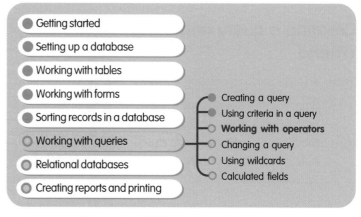

These can be used on any types of value, not just numeric, e.g. '<=M' in a *Surname* field would match surnames beginning with anything from 'A' to 'M'.

AND and OR queries

If two or more criteria must be met, you have an AND query. For example, in a student database, to find students who were over 16 AND played football, you would set '>16' as the criterion in the *Age* field and 'Football' in the *Sports* field. Both criteria must be true for the record to be retrieved. AND can be used to set several criteria in one field, e.g. clients whose last order was after 1/6/03 AND before 30/6/03. You could select these by writing '>1/6/03 AND <30/6/03' in the criteria cell of the *Last order* field.

If either two or more alternative values may be matched, you have an OR query. For example, you could create a query to select clients in Oldcastle or Bridgend. Notice the **or:** row in the query design grid. To set up OR queries, write the first value in the Criteria cell, then the alternative value in the **or:** cell of the same field.

Skill Builder **5.19**

1 Open your *cars.mdb* database.

2 In the **Database** window select *Queries* in the **Objects** bar.

3 Use the wizard to set up a query based on the *Used cars* table to include the *Make, Model, Year, Type* and *Price* fields. Call it 'Newer hatchbacks'.

4 Take the query into **Design** view.

5 Clear the **Show** box of the *Type* field – we do not need to see this.

6 Enter criteria to select hatchbacks from 2002 or later.

7 Click the ❗ Run button.

Changing a query

When it is in datasheet view, a query can be treated as if it were a normal table. You can move, hide and unhide columns, and sort on one or more fields.

These changes will be lost if you run the query again. If you want the results sorted every time, the sort can be written into the query design.

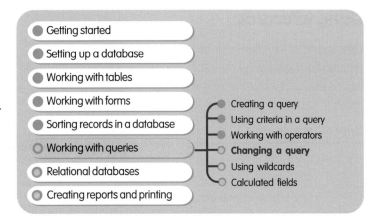

- ● Getting started
- ● Setting up a database
- ● Working with tables
- ● Working with forms
- ● Sorting records in a database
- ○ Working with queries
- ● Relational databases
- ● Creating reports and printing
  - ● Creating a query
  - ● Using criteria in a query
  - ● Working with operators
  - **Changing a query**
  - ○ Using wildcards
  - ○ Calculated fields

Skill Builder 5.20

1 Open your *cars.mdb* database.

2 In the **Database** window select *Queries* in the **Objects** bar.

3 Open the *Newer hatchbacks* query in **Design** view.

4 Set the query to sort the results into descending order of *Year* then *Price*.

5 Click **!**, the **Run** button.

6 Return to **Design** view.

7 Add the *Engine* field, and then drag its column to the left of *Price*.

8 Change the Sort settings so that the results will be in descending order of *Year* then ascending order *Engine* size.

9 Click **!**, the **Run** button.

Your results should look like this

Newer hatchbacks : Select Query

Make	Model	Year	Engine	Price
Nissan	Micra	2004	1	5,999
Nissan	Micra	2004	1.2	6,499
Ford	Ka	2004	1.3	4,599
Nissan	Almera	2004	1.5	7,499
Nissan	Almera	2004	2.2	9,999
Toyota	Yaris	2002	1	3,995
Toyota	Yaris	2002	1.3	7,495
Toyota	Avensis	2002	1.8	6,790
*			0	0	0

Record: |◄| ◄| | 1 | ► | ►| |►*| of 8

Using wildcards

Like expressions allow you to select records through partial matches. An expression should use one or more of these wildcards:

Symbol	stands for
#	any single digit
*	any one or more characters
?	any single character
[ ]	one letter out of the enclosed set

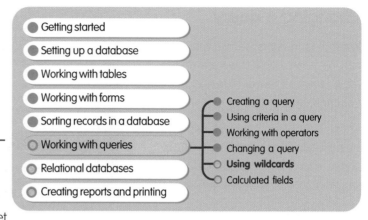

- Getting started
- Setting up a database
- Working with tables
- Working with forms
- Sorting records in a database
- Working with queries
- Relational databases
- Creating reports and printing

- Creating a query
- Using criteria in a query
- Working with operators
- Changing a query
- **Using wildcards**
- Calculated fields

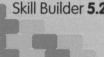

Skill Builder **5.21**

1 Open your *cars.mdb* database.

2 In the **Database** window select *Queries* in the **Objects** bar.

3 Use the wizard to set up a query based on the *Used cars* table to display all the fields. Call it 'wildcards'. Finish in Design view.

4 In the criteria cell for Model, enter "**Mini***". (Do not leave a space after "Mini" – why not?) Click **!**, the **Run** button.

5 Return to **Design** view.

6 Delete the *Model* criteria. Write a Like expression in the *Engine* field that will find all cars with an engine size of 1 and a bit.

7 Click **!**, the **Run** button.

8 Write Like expressions to produce this set of results.

	ID	Make	Model	Engine	Year	Mileage	Type	Price
▶	4	Ford	Ka	1.3	2001	27,000	Hatchback	3,999
	12	Ford	Ka	1.3	2004	16,000	Hatchback	4,599
	20	Citroen	C3	1.4	2002	2,500	Saloon	8,195
	21	Citroen	C3	1.6	2003	16,000	Saloon	7,495
*	(AutoNumber)			0	0	0		0

wildcards : Select Query

Record: I◄ ◄ | 1 | ► ►I ►* of 4

 When creating a query with the wizard, always check that the right table is selected at the first stage.

Calculated fields

A calculated field can draw extra information out of a database. In queries in our *stock* database, for example, we could use a calculate field to show the value of each product line:

Value: [Unit cost] * [No in stock]

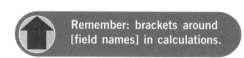

Remember: brackets around [field names] in calculations.

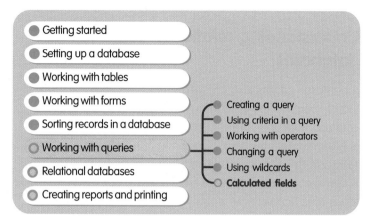

- Getting started
- Setting up a database
- Working with tables
- Working with forms
- Sorting records in a database
- Working with queries
- Relational databases
- Creating reports and printing
  - Creating a query
  - Using criteria in a query
  - Working with operators
  - Changing a query
  - Using wildcards
  - **Calculated fields**

Skill Builder 5.22

1 Open your *cars.mdb* database.

2 In the **Database** window select *Queries* in the **Objects** bar.

3 Use the Wizard to set up a query based on the *Used cars* table to display the *Make, Model, Mileage, Year* and *Price* fields. Call it 'cars by age'. Finish in **Design** view.

4 Create a calculated field to find the age, by subtracting the [Year] from the current year. Call the new field 'Age'. Set up an ascending sort on it.

5 Clear the **Show** box for *Year*.

6 Type a criterion for *Model* to select the saloons.

7 Click **!**, the **Run** button..

The resulting subset should look like this

ID	Make	Model	Mileage	Price	Age
21	Citroen	C3	16,000	7,495	2
20	Citroen	C3	2,500	8,195	3
22	Citroen	Xsara	61,000	2,495	7
2	Ford	Escort	107,000	3,495	9
5	Ford	Mondeo	160,000	650	11
45	Austin	Mini Cooper	70,000	4,395	13
44	Austin	Mini	60,000	995	16
*	ber)		0	0	

Record: 1 of 7

8 Save and close the query.

9 Close the database.

Now try Assignment 5.2

Relational databases

Understanding relational databases

A relational database is one which has two or more tables, which are linked by common data. The link is normally a one-to-many relationship, where one record in the first table is linked to many in the second. Linking tables in this way saves time and reduces errors in data entry, and saves data storage space.

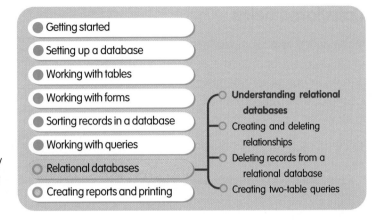

We are going to add a new table to our *stock* database, to hold details of the suppliers. This will be linked to the *Products* table through its *Supplier* field.

Skill Builder 5.23

1 Open your *stock.mdb* database, last saved in Skill Builder 5.11.

2 Create a new table in **Design** view, using the design given below. For each field, enter the name, select the data type, then type in the description.

Field name	Data type	Notes
Supplier ID	Text	Set the field size to 5
Name	Text	Set the field size to 30
Contact	Text	Set the field size to 20
Tel	Text	Set the field size to 15
Discount	Number	Integer

3 Select the *Supplier ID* field and click 🔑 to make it the primary key.

4 Save the table as *Suppliers*.

5 Switch to **Datasheet** view and enter the data shown below.

Supplier ID	Name	Contact	Tel	Discount
CHDOM	China Domestic Goods	Mr Qu	00852 555 7654	5
DUPON	Du Pont Soc	M. Vert	0033 553 23 34 23	10
HKMAN	Hong Kong Manufacturing Co	Ms Lee	00852 555 1234	5
IDEAL	Ideal In Wood	Mr Beech	0061 987 654	10
INTIM	International Imports	Miss Moneypound	0123 456 67	0
SHEFF	Sheffield Fine Steel Ltd	Noah Arkwright	0141 567 4565	5

Creating and deleting relationships

To link the two tables, we must join the *Supplier ID* of the *Suppliers* table to the *Supplier* of the *Products* table.

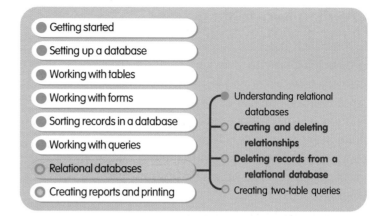

- Getting started
- Setting up a database
- Working with tables
- Working with forms
- Sorting records in a database
- Working with queries
- Relational databases
- Creating reports and printing

  - Understanding relational databases
  - **Creating and deleting relationships**
  - **Deleting records from a relational database**
  - Creating two-table queries

Skill Builder 5.24

1 Open your *stock.mdb* database.

2 Click the ▫ button to open the **Relationships** window.

3 Add the *Suppliers* and *Products* tables, then close the window.

4 The *Products* window will probably be too small to see all the fields. Either scroll down to display the *Supplier*, or enlarge the window.

5 Starting from the *Supplier ID* of the *Suppliers* table, join it to the *Supplier* field of the *Products* table.

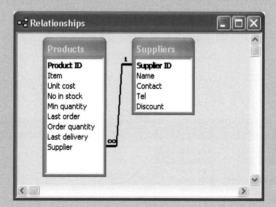

6 In the **Edit Relationships** dialogue box turn on **Enforce Referential Integrity**, then click **Create**.

 Referential Integrity prevents you from deleting a record in a parent table if there are linked records in a child table. It must be turned on to protect your data.

Creating two-table queries

In a relational database, a query can be used to bring together data from more than one table. For example, in our *stock* database, we can use a query to find those items that needed restocking. If the query includes details of the supplier as well as of the products, the resulting subset would have all that was needed to reorder stock.

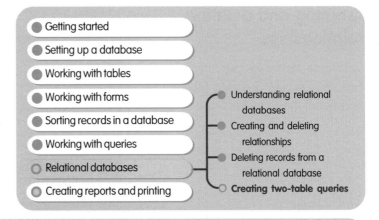

● Getting started
● Setting up a database
● Working with tables
● Working with forms
● Sorting records in a database
● Working with queries
○ Relational databases
○ Creating reports and printing

● Understanding relational databases
● Creating and deleting relationships
● Deleting records from a relational database
○ **Creating two-table queries**

Skill Builder 5.25

1 Open the *stock.mdb* database.

2 Select *Queries* in the **Objects** bar and create a new query using the wizard.

3 Select the *Suppliers* table from the **Tables/Queries** list.

4 Add the *Name*, *Contact* and *Tel* fields to the **Selected Fields**.

5 Select the *Products* table from the **Tables/Queries** list.

6 Add the *Product ID*, *Item*, and *Order quantity* fields to the **Selected Fields**.

7 Work through the rest of the wizard, selecting the Detail layout, and finishing with **Modify the query design**. Call it *Reorder*.

8 At the **Design** window, create a calculated field using the formula [No in stock] - [Min quantity]. Rename it *Need* and set its criteria as <= 0. This will tell us which items need to be reordered.

9 Run the query.

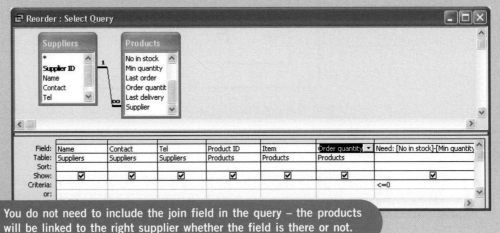

You do not need to include the join field in the query – the products will be linked to the right supplier whether the field is there or not.

Creating reports and printing from databases

Creating a basic report

Tables and forms can be printed, but printouts are normally through reports. In a report, records can be grouped and sorted by one or more fields, e.g. a report could show clients grouped by region, then by town, and listed in alphabetical order of name.

- Getting started
- Setting up a database
- Working with tables
- Working with forms
- Sorting records in a database
- Working with queries
- Relational databases
- Creating reports and printing
  - **Creating a basic report**
  - Formatting a report
  - Creating a report from a query
  - Making changes to a report
  - Introduction to printing
  - Printing database objects
  - Saving data for use in other applications
  - Importing data

Skill Builder **5.26**

1 Open your *cars.mdb* database.

2 Select *Reports* in the **Objects** bar and create a report using the wizard.

3 Select the *Used cars* table from the **Tables/Queries** list.

4 Add all the fields to the **Selected Fields**.

5 At the grouping levels stage, add *Make* then *Model*.

6 Set the report to be sorted by *Engine*, and then by *Year*.

7 Select the stepped, portrait layout, and the Bold style.

8 Give it the title 'Cars by Make and Model'.

9 Finish by previewing the result.

Your report should look like this, and should be just over two pages long

Cars by make and model

Make	Model	Engine	Year	ID	Mileage	Type	Price
Austin							
	Mini						
		1	1989	44	60,000	Saloon	995
	Mini Cooper						
		1.3	1992	45	70,000	Saloon	4,395
Citroen							
	AX						
		1	1996	17	70,000	Hatchback	695
	C3						
		1.4	2002	20	2,500	Saloon	8,195
		1.6	2003	21	16,000	Saloon	7,495
	Saxo						
		1.1	2001	18	17,000	Hatchback	4,795
		1.6	1997	19	42,000	Hatchback	1,695

Formatting a report

The report design can be edited in **Design** view. The techniques are the same as in the **Form Design** view.

Our new report could do with some tweaking – apart from anything else, making it a little more compact would allow it to fit neatly on two pages.

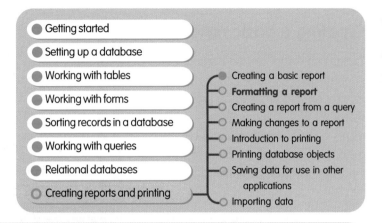

- ● Getting started
- ● Setting up a database
- ● Working with tables
- ● Working with forms
- ● Sorting records in a database
- ● Working with queries
- ● Relational databases
- ○ Creating reports and printing
  - ● Creating a basic report
  - ○ **Formatting a report**
  - ○ Creating a report from a query
  - ○ Making changes to a report
  - ○ Introduction to printing
  - ○ Printing database objects
  - ○ Saving data for use in other applications
  - ○ Importing data

Skill Builder **5.27**

1 Open your *cars.mdb* database.

2 Open the *Cars by Make and Model* report in **Design** view.

3 Change the report header font to Arial – you will need to enlarge the text box – and centre it across the header.

4 Set the colour of the make and model headers to match the report header.

5 Drag the page header divider up slightly to reduce the report header area.

6 Select all the items in the page footer and drag then up to the top of the area, then drag the report footer divider up to reduce the page footer area.

7 Switch to Preview mode to see the new report.

Drag a divider to change the depth of the area above it – note that you cannot drag it up if there is a label, field or anything else in the way

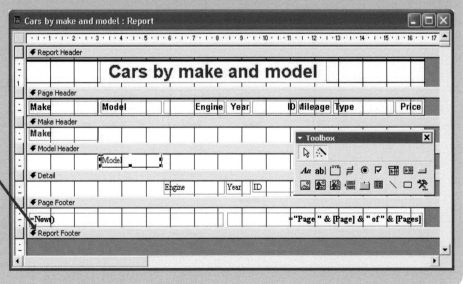

Creating a report from a query

A report can be based on a query instead of a table.

It can contain summary information for any fields which hold numbers.

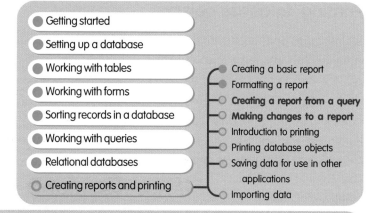

- Getting started
- Setting up a database
- Working with tables
- Working with forms
- Sorting records in a database
- Working with queries
- Relational databases
- Creating reports and printing
  - Creating a basic report
  - Formatting a report
  - **Creating a report from a query**
  - **Making changes to a report**
  - Introduction to printing
  - Printing database objects
  - Saving data for use in other applications
  - Importing data

Skill Builder **5.28**

1 Open your *cars.mdb* database.

2 Using the wizard, create a new report based on the *Saloons* query.

3 Add all the fields to the **Selected Fields**.

4 At the grouping levels, add *Make*, then set the report to be sorted by *Model*.

5 Open the **Summary Options** dialogue box and add the **Sum** and **Avg** to the *Price* field.

6 Set the **Align Left 1** layout and your own choice of style. Leave the title at the default 'Saloons'.

7 Preview the result then switch to **Design** view.

8 Adjust the layout so that the **Avg** and **Sum** displays are on the same line, with the labels close to the values. Preview it again. Is that better?

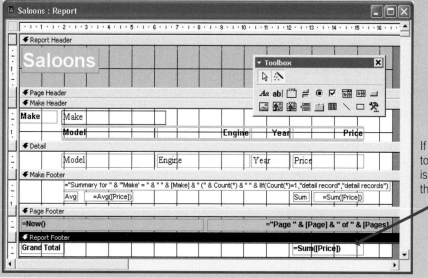

If you use Sum, a grand total for all the records is given at the end of the report

Printing database objects

Tables, forms and reports are all printed in much the same way – you can either get one copy of the complete object by clicking 🖨 or work through the **Print** dialogue box to set options.

Before printing, you can check the output in the **Print preview** and control how it will fit on the paper in the **Page Setup** dialogue box.

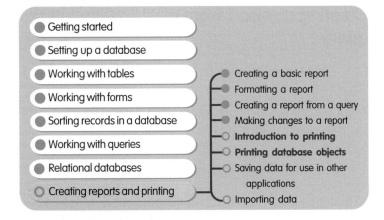

Skill Builder **5.29**

1   Open your *cars.mdb* database.

2   Open the *Cars by make and model* report.

3   Look at all the pages in Print Preview. How does the data fit on the pages? Would different margins settings improve the fit?

4   Open the **Page Setup** dialogue box. On the **Page** tab, make sure that the right paper size is selected. On the **Margins** tab, adjust the margins if necessary.

5   Return to **Print Preview** and check the layout.

6   Use the **Print** dialogue box to print two copies, in colour if possible.

7   Open the *All cars* form. Take it into **Design** view and insert a page number at the bottom left.

8   Check the page setup, then print one copy of pages 3 and 4 of the form.

9   Open the *Used cars* table. Sort it into *Year* order and select those from 2000 and 2001.

10 Print two copies of the selected records.

Saving data for use in other applications

The **Office Links** options provide simple ways to manage the most common links between Office applications – using data from an Access table in a mail merge, and analysing or charting data in Excel.

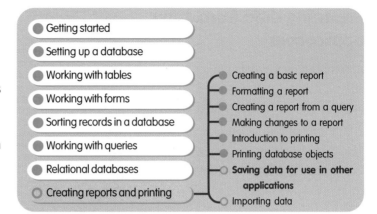

- Getting started
- Setting up a database
- Working with tables
- Working with forms
- Sorting records in a database
- Working with queries
- Relational databases
- Creating reports and printing
  - Creating a basic report
  - Formatting a report
  - Creating a report from a query
  - Making changes to a report
  - Introduction to printing
  - Printing database objects
  - **Saving data for use in other applications**
  - Importing data

Skill Builder 5.30

1 Copy *clients.mdb* from the Resource Bank *Module 5* folder to your work folder and open it.

2 In the Database window, click on the *Client list* table, then select **Merge it with MS Word** from the **Office Links** button.

3 At the wizard, link to the existing document *online orders.doc*.

4 When Word starts, select *Client list* as the table.

5 Insert the *Company name*, *Street* and *Town* fields on three separate lines above the salutation line, and insert the *Contact* after 'Dear...'

6 Click the **View Merged Data** button to see how the merged letters will look. If you have missed out or misplaced fields, correct the errors.

7 Print out two letters.

The letter to Fresh 'n' Fruity should look like this

You can also save the data in a table as a file in a variety of formats, including text and CSV, and any selected item or block of data can be copied from Access and pasted into another Windows application.

United Fruit Markets
Importers & Wholesalers
The Quays
Rivermouth

Fresh 'n' Fruity
12 High Street
Newtown

Dear Mrs Pears

New on-line ordering system

We are delighted to announce our new on-line ordering system. Now you will be able to place your orders with us, at any time of the day or night, through our web site at:

www.unitedfruitmarkets.com/orders

On-line ordering reduces our costs, and we would like to share these savings with you by offering a special 5% discount for on-line orders.

Importing data from other applications

Access can import data produced by other database or spreadsheet applications, as well as files in text, CSV and other formats.

This exercise will create a new table from imported CSV format data.

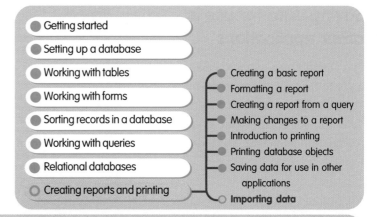

- Getting started
- Setting up a database
- Working with tables
- Working with forms
- Sorting records in a database
- Working with queries
- Relational databases
- Creating reports and printing
  - Creating a basic report
  - Formatting a report
  - Creating a report from a query
  - Making changes to a report
  - Introduction to printing
  - Printing database objects
  - Saving data for use in other applications
  - **Importing data**

Skill Builder **5.31**

1 Start a new blank database.

2 Use the external data import routine to import the file *students.csv* from the Resource Bank *Module 5* folder.

3 The import wizard should split the data into the right fields, but these will need to be named and their properties set. Define the fields as shown here:

Field name	Data type	Field size
ID	Number	Integer
Surname	Text	20
First name	Text	20
Sex	Text	1
Date of Birth	Date/Time	Short date
Course	Text	15
Tutor	Text	15

4 Check that the data has been imported successfully, then save any changes to the design and close the table and the database.

Your table should look like this

	ID	Surname	First name	Sex	Date of Birth	Course	Tutor
	1	Sharma	Rikki	M	04/04/1985	Adv Science	J Brown
	2	Khan	Raxa	F	11/10/1985	Business	P Doig
	3	Green	Peter	M	16/01/1984	Construction	K Smith
	4	Peppit	Ed	M	05/08/1984	Marketing	C Tilley
	5	Lee	May	F	01/05/1985	Business	P Doig
	6	Wright	CD	M	24/09/1984	IT Skills	C Clearly
	7	McCoy	Ian	M	07/06/1985	Construction	K Smith
	8	Smith	Catherine	F	04/02/1985	Marketing	P Doig
	9	de Souza	Jacob	M	11/11/1984	Construction	C Tilley
	10	Tuffery	Elaine	F	08/03/1985	IT Skills	C Clearly
	11	Dubey	Vijay	M	23/09/1984	Construction	K Smith
	12	Gardiner	Tanya	F	07/08/1984	Marketing	P Doig

Students : Table — Record: 12 of 12

 Now try Assignment 5.3

Module 6

PRESENTATIONS

A presentation is a series of slides containing text and images. It can be projected on a screen to an audience, viewed on a PC screen or printed out in several forms.

PowerPoint is the leading presentation software. It is simple to use, but offers a range of sophisticated facilities including:

- ready-made layouts for all kinds of slides
- templates to give a consistent design to a show
- the ability to animate the arrival of items on slides, and the transition from one slide to the next.

- ◎ Using the computer and managing files
- ◎ Word processing
- ◎ Spreadsheets
- ◎ Databases
- ◎ Presentations
- ◎ Information and communication

 Throughout this unit you will be asked to open files that are supplied in the Resource Bank. They can be found on the Resource Bank CD or in the folder which your tutor may have set up for use with this course.

Getting started

The PowerPoint work area

The PowerPoint screen has three panes:

❖ The **Slide** pane is where you build up and display the slides.

❖ The **Slide/Outline** pane shows thumbnails of the slides or their text. Text can be entered or edited, and new slides can be added from here.

❖ The **Notes** pane holds notes that can be printed to accompany the slides.

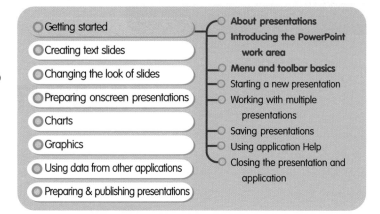

In PowerPoint 2002/2003, Outline view is an option within Normal view – use the tabs to switch between Outline and Slides in the left pane.

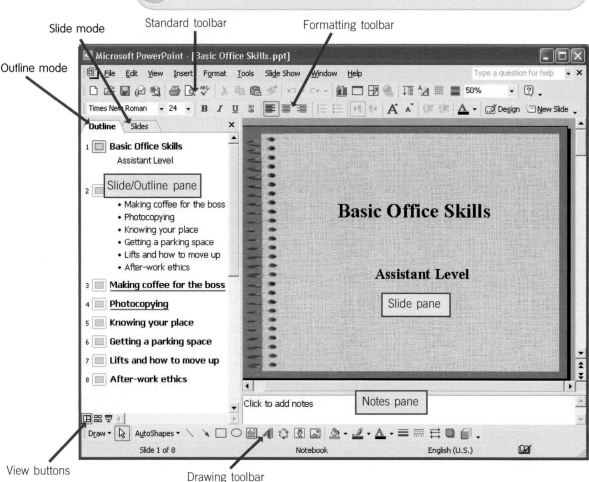

Slide mode

Outline mode

Standard toolbar

Formatting toolbar

View buttons

Drawing toolbar

Starting a new presentation

If you are creating a presentation from scratch, you start with the blank presentation option then add slides one by one.

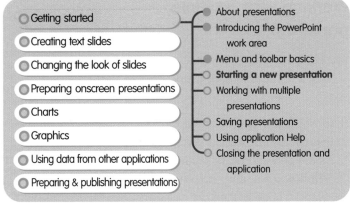

- Getting started
  - About presentations
  - Introducing the PowerPoint work area
  - Menu and toolbar basics
  - **Starting a new presentation**
  - Working with multiple presentations
  - Saving presentations
  - Using application Help
  - Closing the presentation and application
- Creating text slides
- Changing the look of slides
- Preparing onscreen presentations
- Charts
- Graphics
- Using data from other applications
- Preparing & publishing presentations

In PowerPoint 2002/2003 the new presentation and slide layout options are managed in the Task pane.

New Presentation Task Pane

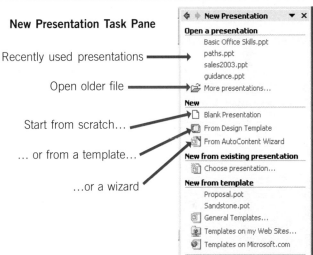

Recently used presentations ⟶

Open older file ⟶

Start from scratch... ⟶

... or from a template... ⟶

...or a wizard ⟶

Skill Builder 6.1

1 Run PowerPoint, either from the **Start** menu or its desktop icon.

2 Open the *Basic Office Skills* presentation in the Resource Bank *Module 6* folder and use this to explore the PowerPoint screen and tools.

3 Start a new blank presentation.

4 Add a new slide – use one of the title slide options.

5 Close the presentation without saving, and close the *Basic Office Skills* presentation.

Working with multiple presentations

You can have several presentations open at once – perhaps to copy material from one to another.

Normally, presentations fill the window, so that you can only see one at a time. To switch between presentations, open the **Window** menu and click on the one you want to bring to the front.

- ○ Getting started
- ○ Creating text slides
- ○ Changing the look of slides
- ○ Preparing onscreen presentations
- ○ Charts
- ○ Graphics
- ○ Using data from other applications
- ○ Preparing & publishing presentations

- ● About presentations
- ● Introducing the PowerPoint work area
- ● Menu and toolbar basics
- ● Starting a new presentation
- ○ **Working with multiple presentations**
- ○ **Saving presentations**
- ○ Using application Help
- ○ Closing the presentation and application

Saving presentations

Always save and name your file at an early stage, and save again regularly – using **File > Save As** if you want to keep a copy or a variation with a different name. Use the same methods as in WordPad (page 17) for a simple save. Change the **Save as type** if you need it in a different format for use by a different application or on a web page.

Skill Builder **6.2**

1   We need two presentations. Open the *Basic Office Skills* presentation, saved in Skill Builder 6.1, and start a new blank presentation, giving it a title slide.

2   Use the **Window** menu to switch between them.

3   Try out the **Cascade** and **Arrange All** options on the **Window** menu.

4   Switch to the new presentation.

5   Save the presentation as *traffic.ppt*. (We'll be adding to this later.)

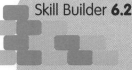

If you are copying material from one presentation to another, **Window > Arrange All** can make this easier. It splits the window between the open presentations – and it works best with only two!

Using application Help

There's plenty of help at hand in PowerPoint, and a choice of easy ways in which to access it.

The quickest way to get help on a topic is to ask the **Assistant** or the **Answer Wizard**.

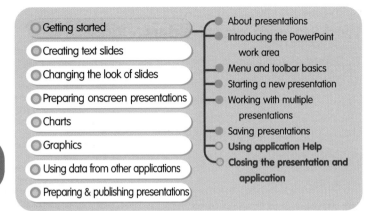

There are a few new features on the Help pages in PowerPoint 2002/2003.

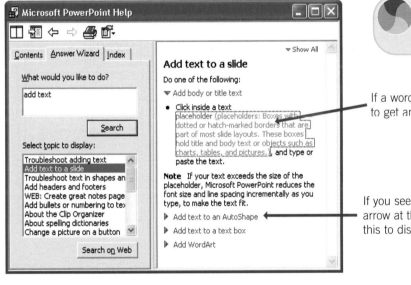

If a word is in blue, click on it to get an explanation (in green)

If you see a blue heading with an arrow at the side, you can click on this to display the text beneath it

Skill Builder **6.3**

1 Open the Help system.

2 Browse through the **Contents** to get an idea of what Help is available.

3 Use the **Assistant** or the **Answer Wizard** to find out how to add text to a slide.

4 Close the Help system.

5 Close all open presentations.

6 Close PowerPoint.

Creating text slides

Working with placeholders

You can start with a blank slide, but it is simpler to begin with a preset slide layout. These have placeholders – areas that have already been formatted – for different types of text and content.

The **text** objects are the title box and bullet lists.

The **content** objects include tables, charts, clip art, organisation charts and media clips.

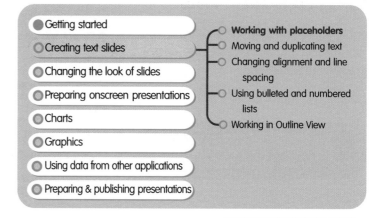

> PowerPoint 2002/2003 has a few more slide layout options than PowerPoint 2000, and the selection is handled in a task pane – unlike a dialogue box, this can be kept open for as long as it is needed, so that you can add any number of slides in one session.

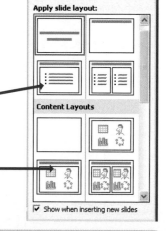

Text layouts

With these you get just the layout, then choose the type of content when the slide opens – there are other layouts set up for specific content objects

 Skill Builder **6.4**

1 Open the *traffic.ppt* presentation that you saved in Skill Builder 6.2.

2 Click into the Title placeholder and enter the text 'Traffic Survey'.

3 Click into the Subtitle placeholder and enter the text 'How people travel to the town centre'.

4 Select the Title placeholder.

5 Format the Title text in bold and give the placeholder a yellow background and a solid blue border.

Traffic Survey
How people travel to the town centre

6 Select the Subtitle placeholder and change the text to Times New Roman.

7 Save the file.

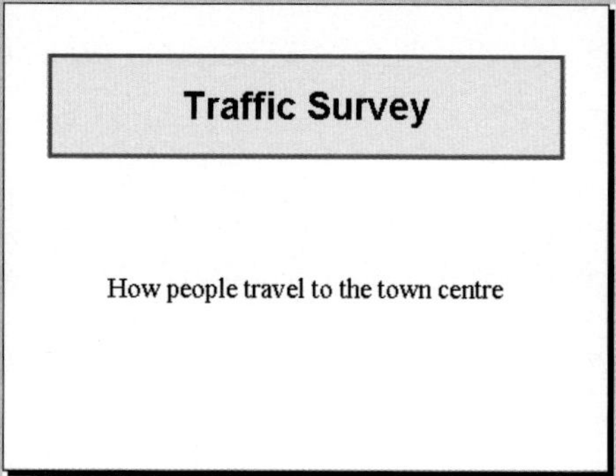

Editing text and layout

Text can be easily moved and duplicated within and between slides using the **Cut/Copy** and **Paste** or **Drag and Drop** techniques. You should never have to type the same text twice.

With the alignment and line spacing options you can fine tune the layout of text on a slide.

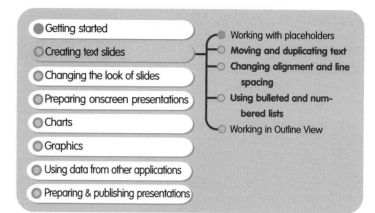

- Getting started
- Creating text slides
- Changing the look of slides
- Preparing onscreen presentations
- Charts
- Graphics
- Using data from other applications
- Preparing & publishing presentations

- Working with placeholders
- **Moving and duplicating text**
- **Changing alignment and line spacing**
- **Using bulleted and numbered lists**
- Working in Outline View

Skill Builder 6.5

1 Open the *traffic.ppt* presentation from Skill Builder 6.4.

2 Use the **New Slide** button to insert a new Title and Text slide.

3 Click into the Title placeholder and enter the text 'Who we asked'. Reselect the placeholder and set the alignment to Left.

4 Click into the Text placeholder and enter the following bullet points.

- 829 people approached
- 329 did not respond
- 243 female respondents
- 257 male respondents
- 500 respondents in total

5 Set the line spacing of the Text placeholder at 0.5 after paragraphs.

6 Set the alignment of the Text placeholder to Middle.

7 Move the bullet points so that they are in the order shown here.

8 Save the file.

Your new slide should look like this

Who we asked

- 500 respondents in total
- 257 male respondents
- 243 female respondents
- 829 people approached
- 329 did not respond

Working in Outline View

If you are simply adding or editing text on your slides, you can do this very efficiently in **Outline** view.

 When a slide is collapsed in Outline view, only the title is visible. Expanding displays the rest of its text again. It can be useful to collapse slides if you want to reorganise them.

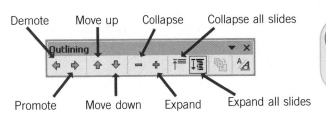

- Getting started
- Creating text slides
- Changing the look of slides
- Preparing onscreen presentations
- Charts
- Graphics
- Using data from other applications
- Preparing & publishing presentations

- Working with placeholders
- Moving and duplicating text
- Changing alignment and line spacing
- Using bulleted and numbered lists
- **Working in Outline View**

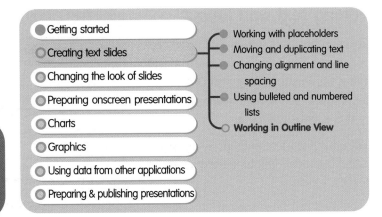

Demote   Move up   Collapse   Collapse all slides

Promote   Move down   Expand   Expand all slides

PowerPoint 2002/2003 has more buttons on the toolbar, and **Demote** and **Promote** are replaced by **Decrease** and **Increase indent** (which do the same jobs).

Skill Builder **6.6**

1 Open the *traffic.ppt* presentation.

2 Switch to **Outline** view and display the **Outlining** toolbar.

3 Insert a new 'Title and Text' slide and give it the title 'Why go to town?'.

4 Enter the following bullet points.
- Work: 165
- Shopping: 214
- Meet friends: 52
- Bank/building society: 26
- Other: 43
  - Pay a bill: 10
  - Looking for work: 27
  - Medical: 6

5 Move 'Shopping' up to become the first bullet point.

6 Demote the last three bullet points.

7 Save the file.

Changing the look of slides

Formatting text

PowerPoint has the same text formatting options as Word, plus a few more. Explore the possibilities!

- ● Getting started
- ● Creating text slides
- ○ Changing the look of slides
- ● Preparing onscreen presentations
- ○ Charts
- ○ Graphics
- ○ Using data from other applications
- ○ Preparing & publishing presentations

- ○ **Formatting text**
- ○ Working with design templates
- ○ Working with master slides
- ○ Adding headers and footers to slides

> In PowerPoint 2002/2003, Font colour is on the Formatting toolbar.

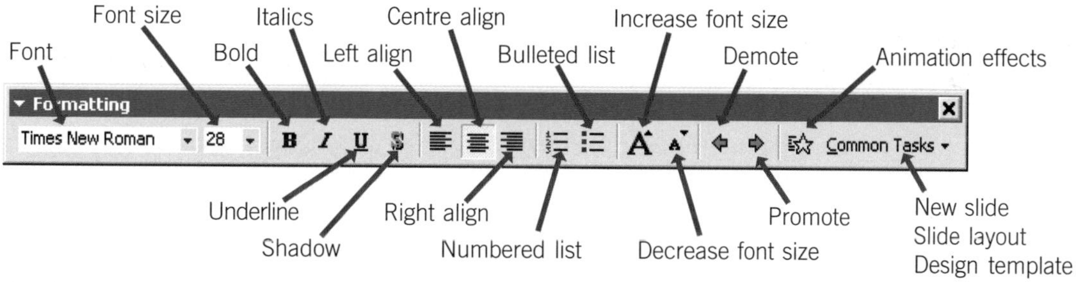

Font | Font size | Italics | Centre align | Increase font size
Bold | Left align | Bulleted list | Demote | Animation effects

Times New Roman ▾ 28 ▾ **B** *I* U S ≣ ≣ ≣ ≣ ≣ A A ⬅ ➡ ⭐ Common Tasks ▾

Underline | Shadow | Right align | Numbered list | Decrease font size | Promote | New slide / Slide layout / Design template

Skill Builder 6.7

1 Open the *traffic.ppt* presentation.

2 Switch to **Slide view** and display the **Drawing** toolbar if it is not visible.

3 Make the following formatting changes to slides 2 and 3.

Make the title text centre aligned, Arial, 44 point, bold, shadowed and coloured red on a yellow background with a 4 point green border.

❖ Make the first level of bullet text Times New Roman, 36 point, black with a picture bullet.

❖ Make the second level of bullet text Times New Roman, 28 point, black with a red round bullet.

4 Save the file.

Slide 3 should now look like this:

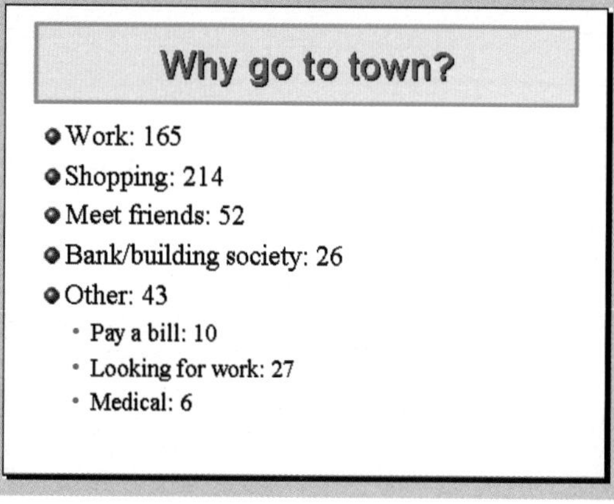

Why go to town?

- ● Work: 165
- ● Shopping: 214
- ● Meet friends: 52
- ● Bank/building society: 26
- ● Other: 43
  - • Pay a bill: 10
  - • Looking for work: 27
  - • Medical: 6

Design templates and master slides

Design templates and master slides give you two ways to sets the default design for your presentation. Unless you change them individually, the slides will use the colours and text formats and display any images set on the template and the master.

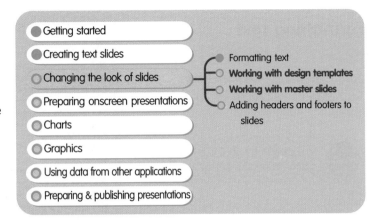

● Getting started

● Creating text slides
  ├ ● Formatting text
● Changing the look of slides
  ├ ○ **Working with design templates**
  ├ ○ **Working with master slides**
● Preparing onscreen presentations
  └ ○ Adding headers and footers to slides

○ Charts

○ Graphics

○ Using data from other applications

○ Preparing & publishing presentations

Skill Builder **6.8**

1   Copy the *Basic Office Skills* presentation from the Resource Bank *Module 6* folder to your work folder, then open your copy.

2   Apply the *Strategic* design template to all the slides.

3   Open the Master Slide and make these changes:

   ❖ Format the title text with Impact or Arial Black, font size 40.

   ❖ Format the first level of bullet text with Courier New, bold.

4   Make these changes to the Title Master:

   ❖ Format the title text with a script font, size 60.

   ❖ Format the subtitle text with Comic Sans, size 36, bold, and add a 3 point border to the text box.

5   Use **File > Save As** to save the file in your work folder.

Slide 2 should now look like this:

Basic Office Skills

   ◆ **Making coffee for the boss**
   ◆ **Knowing your place**
   ◆ **Photocopying**
   ◆ **Lifts and how to move up**
   ◆ **Getting a parking space**
   ◆ **After-work ethics**

   30-Mar-05   Basic Office Skills   2

Check all the slides in the show after changing the template or master slide. The new formatting may result in text not fitting properly on some slides. If this happens, choose a different template, or adjust the formatting on individual slides as required.

Adding headers and footers to slides

You can use the footer to add the date, slide number and the title, your name or any other fixed text to slides.

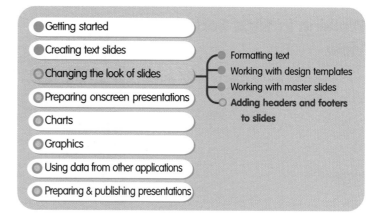

- Getting started
- Creating text slides
- Changing the look of slides
  - Formatting text
  - Working with design templates
  - Working with master slides
  - **Adding headers and footers to slides**
- Preparing onscreen presentations
- Charts
- Graphics
- Using data from other applications
- Preparing & publishing presentations

Skill Builder **6.9**

1 Open the *Basic Office Skills* presentation that you saved in Skill Builder 6.8.

2 Open the **View** menu and select **Header and Footer...**

3 On the **Slide** tab, tick the **Slide number** checkbox.

4 Set the date to **Update automatically**, choosing the short date format.

5 Add the footer text 'Basic Office Skills'.

6 Apply the footer to all the slides and close the dialogue box.

7 Use the Master Slide to format the date, number and footer text, setting the font size to 12.

8 Save the file in your work folder.

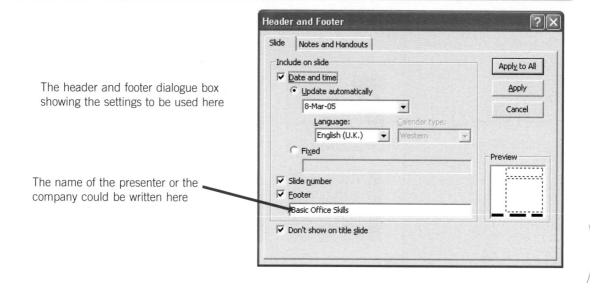

The header and footer dialogue box showing the settings to be used here

The name of the presenter or the company could be written here

Preparing onscreen presentations

Working in Slide Sorter View

If you need to change the order of your slides, the easiest way to do it is by dragging them in **Slide Sorter** view. Slides can also be copied easily here.

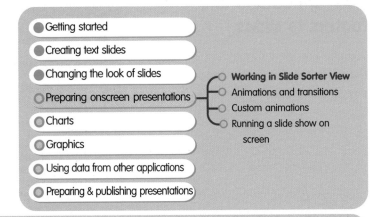

- Getting started
- Creating text slides
- Changing the look of slides
- Preparing onscreen presentations
- Charts
- Graphics
- Using data from other applications
- Preparing & publishing presentations

- **Working in Slide Sorter View**
- Animations and transitions
- Custom animations
- Running a slide show on screen

Skill Builder 6.10

1 Open your copy of the *Basic Office Skills* presentation.

2 Switch to **Slide Sorter** view.

3 Move the '*Knowing your place*' slide to become slide 3.

4 Move the '*Getting a parking space*' slide to become slide 7.

5 Copy Slide 1 to create a new slide 9.

6 Switch to **Normal** or **Outline** view.

7 Edit the order of bullet points on slide 2 so that it matches the order of the slides again.

8 Change the subtitle text on slide 9 to read 'Good luck with your career'.

9 Save the file.

Slide Sorter view gives you a good overview of your presentation

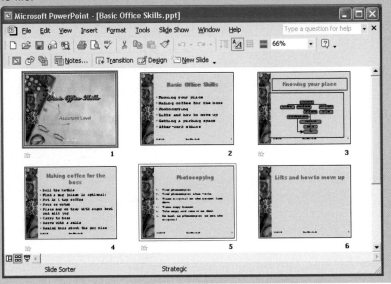

Animations and transitions

Animation controls how the elements of a slide are brought into view. You can specify a different animation for every slide or apply one style to the whole set.

Transition controls how the show progresses from one slide to another. If none are set, each slide simply replaces the previous one.

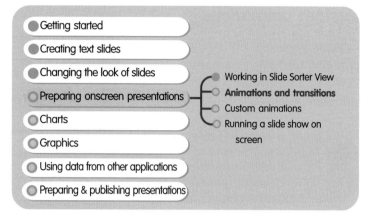

 In PowerPoint 2002/2003, animation and transitions are set in the Task Pane, and in a slightly different way. Here's how.

1 Open the **Slide Show** menu and select **Slide Transition**.

2 Select the slides which are to have an animation.

3 In the **Slide Transition** Task Pane, click on a style and set the **Modify** options to apply it to the selected slide or click **Apply to All Slides**.

The process is the same for animations, except that they did not have optional settings.

The **Slide Transition** Task Pane in PowerPoint 2002/2003

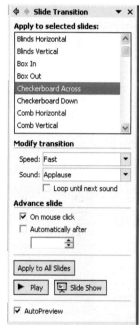

Skill Builder 6.11

1 Open your copy of the *Basic Office Skills* presentation.

2 Switch to **Slide Sorter** view.

3 Set a suitable animation on slide 1 to start the show, and one on slide 2 that will bring on each bullet point separately.

4 Apply one transition style to all the slides in the presentation.

5 Save the file.

Custom animations

Every element on a slide can be animated separately – in PowerPoint 2002/2003, every bullet point can be animated separately!

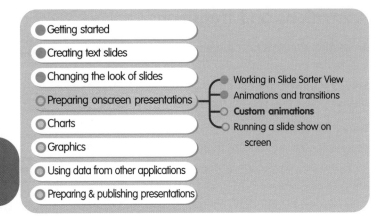

- Getting started
- Creating text slides
- Changing the look of slides
- Preparing onscreen presentations
  - Working in Slide Sorter View
  - Animations and transitions
  - **Custom animations**
  - Running a slide show on screen
- Charts
- Graphics
- Using data from other applications
- Preparing & publishing presentations

To animate individual bullet points in PowerPoint 2002/2003, you must first apply an animation scheme to the slide.

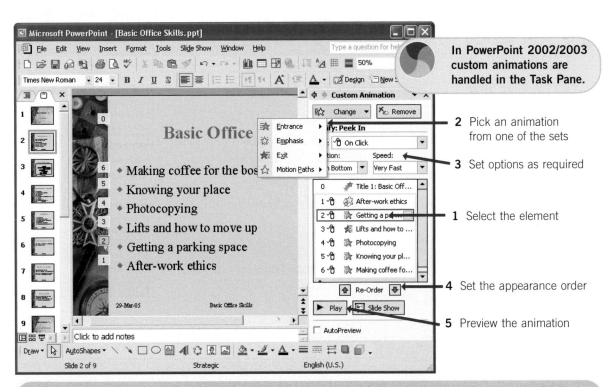

In PowerPoint 2002/2003 custom animations are handled in the Task Pane.

2 Pick an animation from one of the sets

3 Set options as required

1 Select the element

4 Set the appearance order

5 Preview the animation

Skill Builder **6.12**

1 Open your copy of the *Basic Office Skills* presentation.

2 Switch to **Normal** view.

3 Select a slide.

4 Open the dialogue box/task pane with **Slide Show > Custom Animation...**

5 Explore the possibilities of custom animations.

6 If you've overdone things, don't save the file!

Running a slide show on screen

Before running your slide show, go to the **Set Up Show** dialogue box to set the show options.

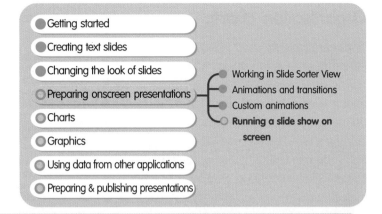

- Getting started
- Creating text slides
- Changing the look of slides
- Preparing onscreen presentations
  - Working in Slide Sorter View
  - Animations and transitions
  - Custom animations
  - **Running a slide show on screen**
- Charts
- Graphics
- Using data from other applications
- Preparing & publishing presentations

Skill Builder 6.13

1 Open your copy of the *Basic Office Skills* presentation.

2 Open the **Slide Show** menu and select **Set Up Show...**

3 Set the **Show type** to **Presented by a speaker**.

4 In the **Show slides** area, set it to display from slides 1 to 5.

5 Set the **Advance slides** option to **Manually**.

6 Click **OK**.

7 Select slide 1, go to **Slide Show** view, then click your way through the show.

Photocopying

1. Find photocopier
2. Find photocopier that works
3. Place original on the screen face down
4. Press copy button
5. Take copy and return to desk

You can navigate to any slide via the pop-up menu

| Next |
| Previous |
| Go ▶ |
| Meeting Minder... |
| Speaker Notes |
| Pointer Options ▶ |
| Screen ▶ |
| Help |
| End Show |

| Slide Navigator |
| By Title ▶ |
| Custom Show ▶ |
| Previously Viewed |

| 1 Basic Office Skills |
| 2 Basic Office Skills |
| 3 Knowing your place |
| 4 Making coffee for the boss |
| ✓ 5 Photocopying |
| Slide Navigator |

Now try Assignment 6.1

Charts

Organisation charts

These are typically used to illustrate the structure of an organisation. A chart consists of boxes containing the names and/or titles of the staff, linked to show the nature of the relationships. The starting shape has a boss plus three staff. You can change these or add boxes for different types of relationships.

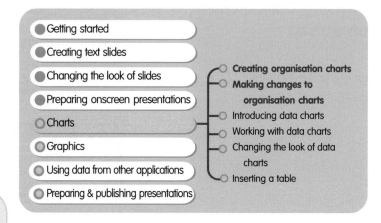

- Getting started
- Creating text slides
- Changing the look of slides
- Preparing onscreen presentations
- Charts
- Graphics
- Using data from other applications
- Preparing & publishing presentations

- **Creating organisation charts**
- **Making changes to organisation charts**
- Introducing data charts
- Working with data charts
- Changing the look of data charts
- Inserting a table

 In PowerPoint 2002/2003 organisation charts are produced quite differently – here's how.

Organisation charts in PowerPoint 2002/2003

1 Start with the slide layout *Title and Diagram or Organization Chart*.

2 When the slide apears, double-click the icon.

3 At the **Design Gallery**, select **Organization Chart**.

4 The initial layout has one top level box with three beneath it. Each box has a '*Click to add text*' prompt. Replace this with your own text – type as many lines as are needed.

5 To add a new box, click on the one to which it will be linked. On the **Organization Chart** toolbar, click **Insert Shape** and select the relationship. Repeat to add another box at the same point.

6 To delete an unwanted box, select it and press **[Delete]**.

7 To format text, select the whole box, or some text within it, and use the normal formatting tools.

8 To change the colour or style of the boxes or lines, use the tools on the **Drawing** toolbar.

9 When you have finished, click on the background of the slide.

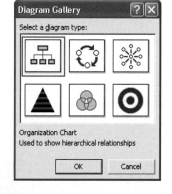

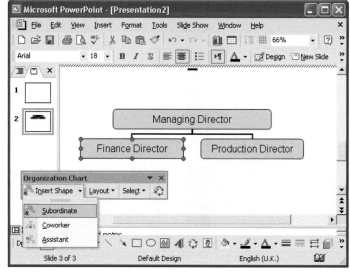

Skill Builder **6.14**

1 Start a new presentation.

2 Add a new slide, with a title and organisation chart.

3 Give it the title 'Company Structure'.

4 Replace the text in the top level box with 'Managing Director', then type 'Finance Director' and 'Production Director' in the first two boxes below.

5 Delete the empty second level box.

6 Add two boxes below the Finance Director. Replace the prompt in one with 'HR director (vacancy)', typed on two lines and the other with 'Accountant'.

7 Add two boxes below the Production Director, labelling them 'Production Manager' and 'Sales Manager'.

8 Format the text as follows:

> Top level: Impact, 18 point
>
> Second level: Arial, bold, 16 point
>
> Third level: Arial, 14 point

9 Format the boxes as follows:

> Top level: yellow, with shadow
>
> Second level: orange, with shadows

10 Set the connecting lines, to 3 point, red.

11 Switch to **Normal** view to see the completed slide.

12 Save the presentation as *OrgChart.ppt*.

Your finished organisation chart should look like this:

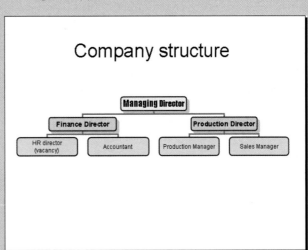

 To apply the same formatting to several elements, select them as a group by holding **[Shift]** while you click on them, then set the font, colour, or other options.

Data charts

Excel charts and worksheets can be inserted into a slide – either created from new or from existing files – but if you have a small set of data to chart, it is simpler to use the Chart facility.

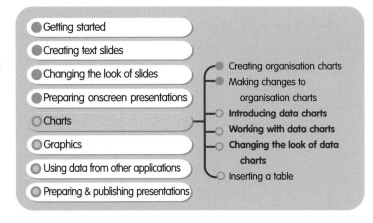

- Getting started
- Creating text slides
- Changing the look of slides
- Preparing onscreen presentations
- Charts
- Graphics
- Using data from other applications
- Preparing & publishing presentations
  - Creating organisation charts
  - Making changes to organisation charts
  - **Introducing data charts**
  - **Working with data charts**
  - **Changing the look of data charts**
  - Inserting a table

Skill Builder **6.15**

1 Open your *traffic.ppt* presentation, last saved in Skill Builder 6.7.

2 Add a slide, using the layout with a **Chart** object and double-click .

3 Give it the title 'How people travel'. Format this to match the other titles.

4 Enter this data into the datasheet.

	Work	Shops	Friends	Bank	Other
Car	96	104	10	19	6
Bus	28	68	12	4	27
Walk	36	36	26	1	9
Cycle	5	6	4	2	1

5 Close the datasheet when you have finished.

6 Change the colours of the bars to red, blue, green and yellow, and give the chart area a thick green border.

7 Change the font of the legend and category axis to Tahoma, 16 point.

8 Switch to **Normal** view.

9 Save the file.

The chart slide should look like this:

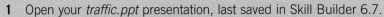

Inserting a table

If you need to present data in rows and columns – use a table. The table and border tools are the same as in Word (see page 44).

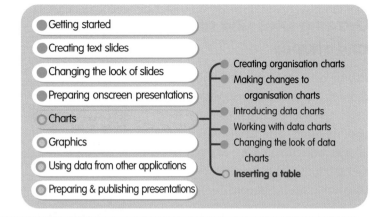

Getting started
Creating text slides
Changing the look of slides
Preparing onscreen presentations
Charts
Graphics
Using data from other applications
Preparing & publishing presentations

Creating organisation charts
Making changes to organisation charts
Introducing data charts
Working with data charts
Changing the look of data charts
Inserting a table

Skill Builder **6.16**

1 Open your *traffic.ppt* presentation.

2 Add a slide, using the layout with a **Table** object and double-click .

3 Set the table size to 3 columns and 4 rows.

4 Type 'Car parks' as the title and format it to match the other titles.

5 Enter this data into the table:

Car park	Capacity	24 hour?
Central	790	Y
Station	245	N
Highpoint	650	N

6 Set the line thickness to 4½ and the colour to green, then drop down the **Borders** palette and click to apply the settings to the outside border.

7 Click on the background of the slide to deselect the table.

8 Save the file.

To define a border, set the style, weight and colour first, then pick the border to apply the settings to

Car parks

Car park	Capacity	24 hour?
Central	790	Y
Station	245	N
Highpoint	650	N

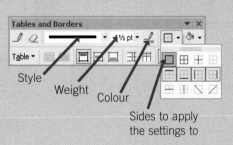

Style
Weight
Colour
Sides to apply the settings to

Graphics

Drawing lines and arrows and shapes

PowerPoint has a good set of tools for drawing lines, arrows, rectangles, ovals and other shapes. If you have the time and the ability, you can create complex images with these tools – and any of us can produce simple but effective diagrams and illustrations.

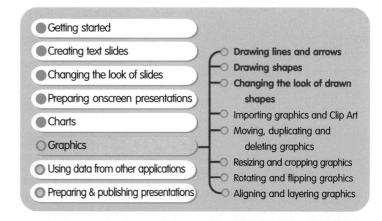

Skill Builder **6.17**

1 Start a new presentation. On slide 1, type the title 'Graphics' and the subtitle 'In PowerPoint'.

2 Add a slide, containing only a title placeholder.

3 Use the tools on the **Drawing** toolbar to create a diagram showing the main inputs to and outputs from the processor in a PC.

Input devices: keyboard, mouse

Output devices: monitor, printer, speakers

Input/output devices: disk drives

4 Save the file as *graphics*.

Your drawing should have these elements, but may look very different from mine

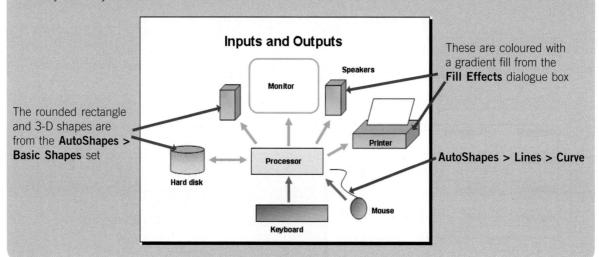

The rounded rectangle and 3-D shapes are from the **AutoShapes > Basic Shapes** set

These are coloured with a gradient fill from the **Fill Effects** dialogue box

AutoShapes > Lines > Curve

Graphics and Clip Art

Images can add impact to your presentations – people normally remember pictures better than words.

Importing Clip Art is different in PowerPoint 2002/2003, but once it is there, the techniques are the same as in PowerPoint 2000.

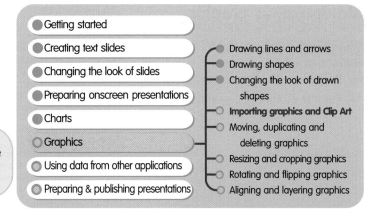

- ● Getting started
- ● Creating text slides
- ● Changing the look of slides
- ● Preparing onscreen presentations
- ● Charts
- ○ Graphics
- ○ Using data from other applications
- ○ Preparing & publishing presentations

- Drawing lines and arrows
- Drawing shapes
- Changing the look of drawn shapes
- ○ **Importing graphics and Clip Art**
- ○ Moving, duplicating and deleting graphics
- ○ Resizing and cropping graphics
- ○ Rotating and flipping graphics
- ○ Aligning and layering graphics

Importing Clip Art in PowerPoint 2002/2003

1 Start from a slide with a Clip Art placeholder.

2 Double-click the icon.

3 The **Select Picture** dialogue box will open.

4 Type one or more words to describe what you are looking for and click **Search**.

5 Scroll through the matching images.

6 To insert an image, double-click on it.

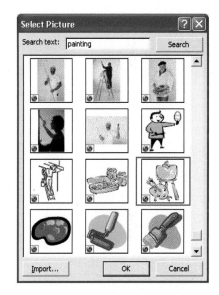

 shows that the picture is on the hard disk – if the icon is not there, you will need the Clip Art CD-ROM

Skill Builder **6.18**

1 Open your *graphics.ppt* presentation.

2 Add a new slide, using a Layout with a Clip Art object.

3 Insert a Clip Art image of a scanner or a camera.

4 Copy the image, then paste it into the slide with the Inputs and Outputs diagram.

5 Resize the image to match the drawn objects.

6 Move the image and/or drawn objects as necessary to fit the image into the diagram. Add a text box caption.

7 Save the file.

Manipulating graphics

Imported pictures and clip art can be edited and adjusted using the tools on the **Picture** toolbar and the options in the **Format Picture** dialogue box.

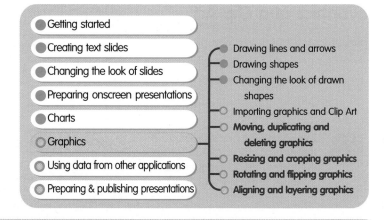

Skill Builder 6.19

1. Open your *graphics.ppt* presentation.

2. Add a new blank slide.

3. Add a text box. Type in 'Imported graphics', and format the font and the box to create a bright and bold title.

4. Use **Insert > Picture > From File...** to insert the image *drawing.bmp* from the Resource Bank *Module 6* folder – it is the screenshot from page 146!

5. Stretch the image to almost fill the slide, then crop off its edges.

6. If the image overlaps the text box, send it to the back.

7. Save the file.

Cropping an image – the dotted line shows where the image will be cropped to

The Crop tool

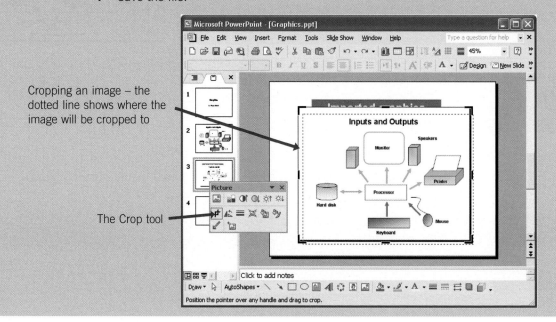

Using data from other applications

Duplicating and importing data

Data can be copied easily between PowerPoint and other Office applications, and usually copied between it and any other Windows applications.

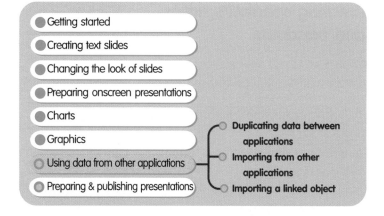

- Getting started
- Creating text slides
- Changing the look of slides
- Preparing onscreen presentations
- Charts
- Graphics
- Using data from other applications
- Preparing & publishing presentations

- Duplicating data between applications
- Importing from other applications
- Importing a linked object

Skill Builder 6.20

1 Open the *traffic.ppt* presentation.

2 Add a new slide containing only a title text box.

3 Start Excel and open the file *cartrips.xls*.

4 Copy the text from cell A1. (See the tip!)

5 Switch to your presentation and paste the text into the title.

6 Return to the spreadsheet and copy the chart.

7 Switch back to PowerPoint and paste the chart in as a linked object.

8 Enlarge the chart to fill the slide.

9 Format the title to match the titles on the other slides.

10 Save the file.

When copying text from a spreadsheet, you must go into the cell and highlight the text to select it to copy it successfully. Do not simply copy the cell – try it and you will see why.

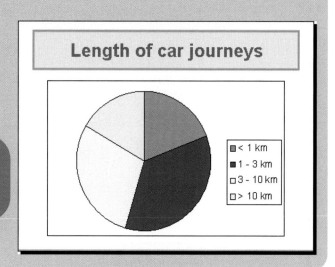

Length of car journeys

- ■ < 1 km
- ■ 1 - 3 km
- □ 3 - 10 km
- □ > 10 km

Preparing and publishing presentations

Creating speaker's notes and handouts

If you want to give your audience some printed material, you could give them:

❖ a notes page, showing the slide and its notes, printed one slide per page

❖ a handout, showing 2, 3, 4, 6 or 9 slides to a page.

- Getting started
- Creating text slides
- Changing the look of slides
- Preparing onscreen presentations
- Charts
- Graphics
- Using data from other applications
- Preparing & publishing presentations
  - Checking your presentation for spelling errors
  - **Creating speaker's notes and handouts**
  - Printing slides
  - Changing your personal settings

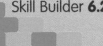

Skill Builder 6.21

1 Start Word and open the *traffic notes* file in the Resource Bank *Module 6* folder. This contains notes to be copied into the presentation.

2 Return to PowerPoint and open the *traffic* presentation. Access the **Notes Master** and increase the font size to 14 point.

3 Switch to Word.

4 Copy the text beneath the 'Slide 1' heading.

5 Switch to PowerPoint and make sure you are using **Normal** view.

6 Select Slide 1 and click into its **Notes pane**. Paste in the notes.

7 Repeats steps 3 to 6 for each of the remaining slides.

8 Go to **Notes Pane** view to see how the pages will look when printed. Check that the notes are the right ones for the slides!

9 Save the file.

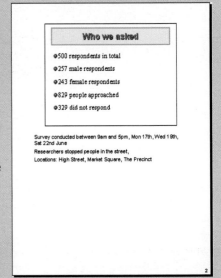

> Always spell check your presentations, and proof read them carefully before showing them.

Printing slides

In PowerPoint you can print:

❖ the slides, as they appear on screen

❖ the notes, by themselves

❖ the slides with notes as handouts

❖ the presentation's text, as an outline.

You can also select which slides to include and how many copies.

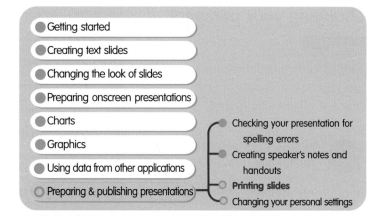

- ● Getting started
- ● Creating text slides
- ● Changing the look of slides
- ● Preparing onscreen presentations
- ● Charts
- ● Graphics
- ● Using data from other applications
- ○ Preparing & publishing presentations
  - ● Checking your presentation for spelling errors
  - ● Creating speaker's notes and handouts
  - ○ **Printing slides**
  - ○ Changing your personal settings

In PowerPoint 2002/2003, there is a Print Preview facility that will show you how the pages will look when printed – whether as slides, handouts, notes pages or outline.

Skill Builder **6.22**

1 Open your *traffic.ppt* presentation.

2 Check the outline and ensure that all the slides are expanded.

3 Using the **Print** dialogue box, print the following:

  1 copy each of slides 1, 3 and 5, as slides

  2 copies of the presentation as handouts, with 6 slides to the page

  1 copy each of slides 2 and 4 as notes pages

  1 copy of the whole presentation in outline view.

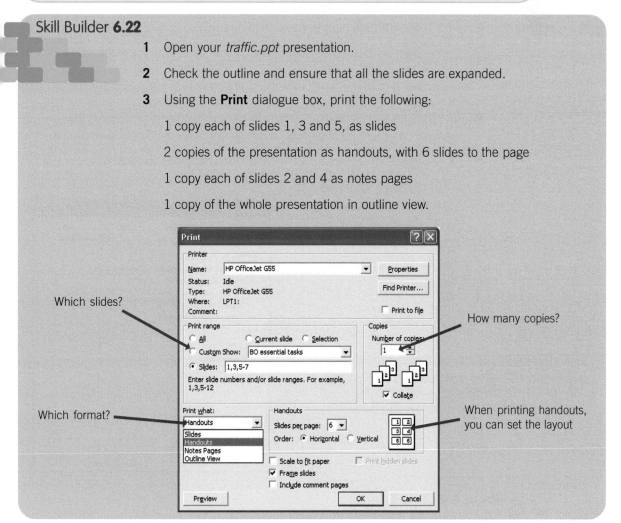

Which slides?

Which format?

How many copies?

When printing handouts, you can set the layout

Changing your personal settings

Take a few minutes to set the options to suit your way of working – it will save you time and effort in the future.

In PowerPoint 2002/2003 there is also a Security tab where you can set a password and add other protection.

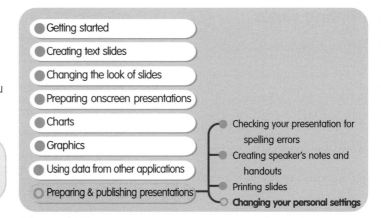

- Getting started
- Creating text slides
- Changing the look of slides
- Preparing onscreen presentations
- Charts
- Graphics
- Using data from other applications
- Preparing & publishing presentations
  - Checking your presentation for spelling errors
  - Creating speaker's notes and handouts
  - Printing slides
  - **Changing your personal settings**

Skill Builder **6.23**

1 Open the **Options** dialogue box.

2 On the **General** tab, type your name and initials.

3 On the **Edit** tab look at the settings and think about how you normally work, e.g. when importing charts, do you want to keep their Excel formatting or take the PowerPoint fonts?

4 On the **Print** tab, you can choose to define settings to use when doing a simple Print, instead of using the most recent ones as you normally would.

5 On the **Save** tab set the default location for saving your presentations.

6 On the **Spelling and style** tab, turn on the **Check spelling as you type** option if you want PowerPoint to pick up errors as they occur.

7 Click **OK** to close the dialogue box and save your new settings.

If you do not know what an option does or how it affects things, leave it at the default setting.

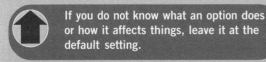

Now try Assignment 6.2

Module 7

INFORMATION AND COMMUNICATION

The Internet and the Web are not the same thing. The *Internet* is a world-wide network of computers, linked by public and private telephone lines, cables and satellite links. The Web is one way in which people use the Internet. It consists of hundreds of millions of *Web sites* containing billions of *pages* of information, stored on computers throughout the world.

Email (*electronic mail*) is the second major use of the Internet. With email you can send plain messages, or attach graphics, documents or other files to them. It can be an efficient way to communicate. Delivery is fast, with messages normally arriving in the mailbox in a few minutes.

- ⦿ Using the computer and managing files
- ⦿ Word processing
- ⦿ Spreadsheets
- ⦿ Databases
- ⦿ Presentations
- ◯ Information and communication

 Throughout this unit you will be asked to open files that are supplied in the Resource Bank. They can be found on the Resource Bank CD or in the folder which your tutor may have set up for use with this course.

Getting started with the Internet and the Web

Web browsers and URLs

Every web page has its own address, or URL (Uniform Resource Locator). This may simply be the name of the web site, e.g. **www.microsoft.com** or identify a page at that site, and it may include the path through the folders at the site. There may also be further details at the end. If only the site name is given, the browser goes to the home page at the site.

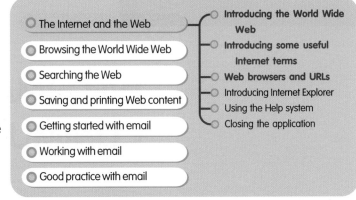

- The Internet and the Web
  - Introducing the World Wide Web
- Browsing the World Wide Web
  - Introducing some useful Internet terms
- Searching the Web
  - Web browsers and URLs
- Saving and printing Web content
  - Introducing Internet Explorer
- Getting started with email
  - Using the Help system
- Working with email
  - Closing the application
- Good practice with email

You may see 'http://' at the start of a URL. This stands for HyperText Transfer Protocol and identifies the URL as a web page. You can omit it when you type a URL.

A typical URL

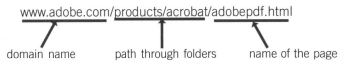

www.adobe.com/products/acrobat/adobepdf.html

domain name path through folders name of the page

Skill Builder 7.1

1 Launch Internet Explorer from the **Start** menu or the desktop icon.

2 Click into the Address bar and delete the address that is there already.

3 Get today's news from the BBC by typing in this address:

    news.bbc.co.uk

4 Find out the weather at MSN, by typing in this address:

    www.msn.co.uk/news/weather/default.asp

Addresses must be typed correctly, but are not case-sensitive – WWW.LYCOS.CO.UK works just as well as www.lycos.co.uk. Watch for symbols. Some addresses include a tilde (~). The address for the top page of a site may end with a slash (/), though this can be omitted.

Internet Explorer

To access the World Wide Web, you need a web browser – a program that can display Web pages and interpret the links that will take you from one page to another. Internet Explorer is the browser supplied with Windows. Run it from the **Start** menu or from its desktop icon.

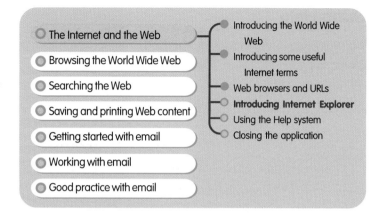

- The Internet and the Web
  - Introducing the World Wide Web
  - Introducing some useful Internet terms
  - Web browsers and URLs
  - **Introducing Internet Explorer**
  - Using the Help system
  - Closing the application
- Browsing the World Wide Web
- Searching the Web
- Saving and printing Web content
- Getting started with email
- Working with email
- Good practice with email

Explorer bar – used when searching the Internet or using Favorites or History

The **Address bar** shows you where you are. You can type a URL here to go to a page.

Typed addresses are stored in the drop-down list

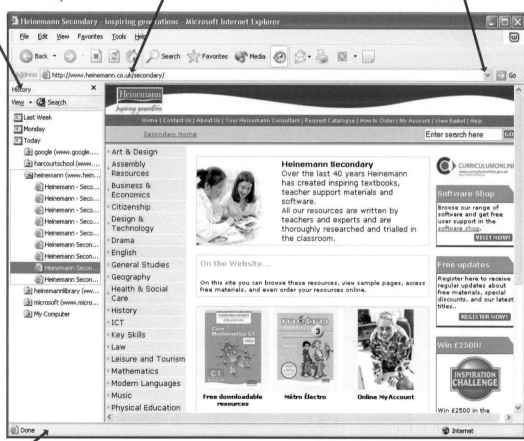

The **Status bar** at the bottom of the page shows how much of an incoming file has been loaded.

 When Internet Explorer starts, it first goes to the home page – this might be at MSN, or your Internet Sevice Provider's site, or a page selected by your organisation. You can choose your own home page through the Internet Options dialogue box (reach this from the Tools menu).

Using Help

The Help system in Internet Explorer is similar to that in the Office applications, once you get into it.

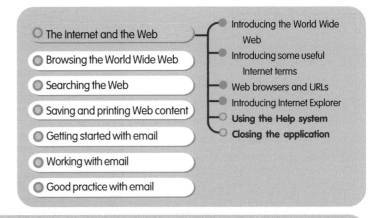

- ○ The Internet and the Web
  - ● Introducing the World Wide Web
  - ● Introducing some useful Internet terms
  - ● Web browsers and URLs
  - ● Introducing Internet Explorer
  - ○ **Using the Help system**
  - ○ **Closing the application**
- ● Browsing the World Wide Web
- ● Searching the Web
- ● Saving and printing Web content
- ● Getting started with email
- ● Working with email
- ● Good practice with email

Skill Builder **7.2**

1 Use **Help > Contents and Index** to open the Help system.

2 Bring the **Contents** tab to the front.

3 In the section 'Finding the Web Pages You Want', read the Help on changing the home page.

4 Use the information to change your home page, ready for your next session.

5 Close the Help system.

6 Close Internet Explorer.

7 If you use a dial-up connection, make sure that it is disconnected.

Help window tools

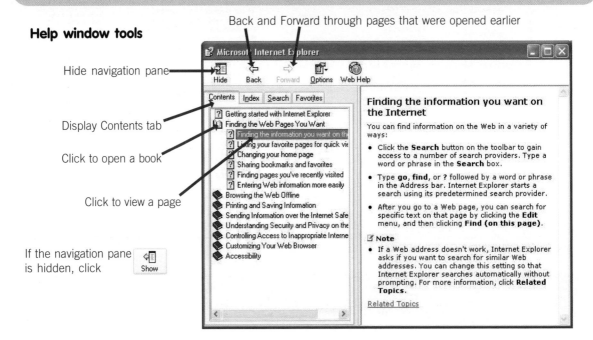

Back and Forward through pages that were opened earlier

Hide navigation pane

Display Contents tab

Click to open a book

Click to view a page

If the navigation pane is hidden, click Show

Browsing the World Wide Web

Surfing the Web

Once you have got started, you can explore the Web by following hypertext links from page to page. Links are easy to spot. Text with a link is underlined and usually blue. When you point to an image or text with a link, the cursor turns into 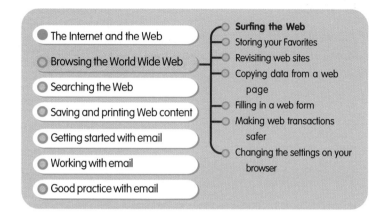 and the address of the page is shown in the **Status** bar.

Click on the link to go to its page.

- The Internet and the Web
- Browsing the World Wide Web
- Searching the Web
- Saving and printing Web content
- Getting started with email
- Working with email
- Good practice with email

- **Surfing the Web**
- Storing your Favorites
- Revisiting web sites
- Copying data from a web page
- Filling in a web form
- Making web transactions safer
- Changing the settings on your browser

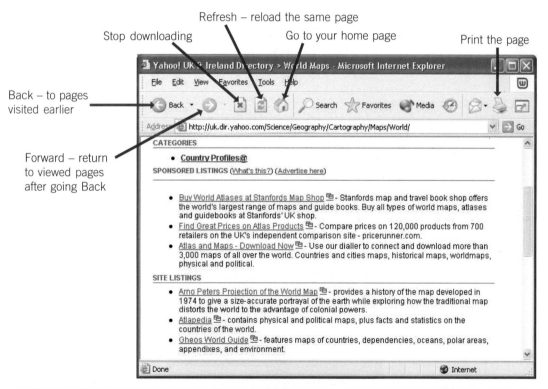

Stop downloading

Refresh – reload the same page

Go to your home page

Print the page

Back – to pages visited earlier

Forward – return to viewed pages after going Back

Skill Builder **7.3**

1   Go to Yahoo at this address:

   uk.yahoo.com

2   Go down to the Web Site Directory and follow the link to Maps, then go on from there to find World maps.

3   Find a site that has a physical map of Peru.

Favorites

If you want a permanent link to a page, add it to your Favorites. You can then get back to it with a simple click.

- The Internet and the Web
- Browsing the World Wide Web
- Searching the Web
- Saving and printing Web content
- Getting started with email
- Working with email
- Good practice with email

- Surfing the Web
- **Storing your Favorites**
- Revisiting web sites
- Copying data from a web page
- Filling in a web form
- Making web transactions safer
- Changing the settings on your browser

Skill Builder 7.4

1 Find a site that you will want to revisit.

2 Click ☆ Favorites to open **Favorites** in the Explorer bar.

3 Click 📑 Add... .

4 In the **Add Favorite** dialogue box, edit the name, if necessary.

5 To add to the main list, simply click **OK**.

6 To store the Favorite in a folder, click Create in >> to fully open the box, select the folder and click **OK**.

Add the page to your Favorites

Click to open/ close a folder

Click to go to the page

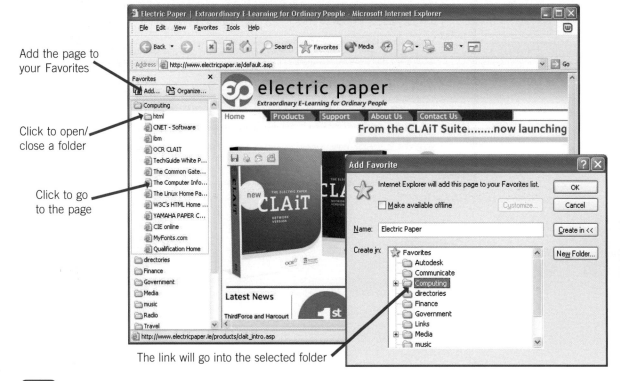

The link will go into the selected folder

Revisiting web sites

The History facility enables you to revisit sites easily, but it takes up disk space. If you visit a lot of sites, but rarely go back to the same one, then much of the History will be wasted.

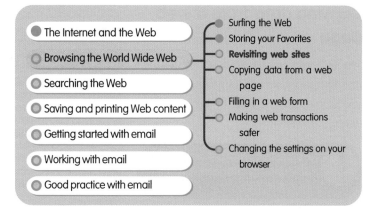

- The Internet and the Web
- Browsing the World Wide Web
- Searching the Web
- Saving and printing Web content
- Getting started with email
- Working with email
- Good practice with email

- Surfing the Web
- Storing your Favorites
- **Revisiting web sites**
- Copying data from a web page
- Filling in a web form
- Making web transactions safer
- Changing the settings on your browser

Skill Builder 7.5

1   Open the History list in the Explorer bar.

2   Use the History links – if they are there – to revisit a selected page on any site that you visited when you were last online

3   Click the **View** button and select **By Order Visited Today**. You should see every page that you have visited, with the most recent at the top.

4   Display the History list in site order.

5   Open the **Internet Options** dialogue box and set number of days that History is stored to suit your way of working. (If you often revisit sites days or weeks later, and you have plenty of hard disk space, set this to 20 or 30 days. If you want to save space, or do not revisit sites except during the same session, set it to 2 or 3 days.)

Watch the Address bar when typing in an URL – if you have been there before, the address may be completed for you.

Copying data from a web page

The text and images from Web pages can be copied into documents – it is one of the reasons why the Web is so useful for research.

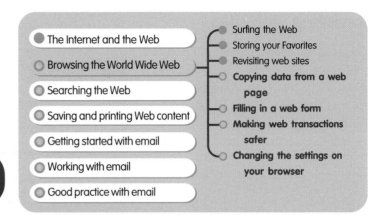

- ● The Internet and the Web
  - ● Surfing the Web
  - ● Storing your Favorites
  - ● Revisiting web sites
- ○ Browsing the World Wide Web
  - ○ **Copying data from a web page**
  - ○ **Filling in a web form**
  - ○ **Making web transactions safer**
  - ○ **Changing the settings on your browser**
- ○ Searching the Web
- ○ Saving and printing Web content
- ○ Getting started with email
- ○ Working with email
- ○ Good practice with email

Respect copyright! Always acknowledge any work copied from the Web.

Skill Builder 7.6

1   Go to the National Gallery at www.nationalgallery.org.uk.

2   Go to the **Collections** area and locate the Sunflowers by Van Gogh – if you cannot see a link, use the **Search** facility to find it.

3   Start Word and open a new document.

4   Copy the image and the descriptive text, separately, into Word

5   Set the text wrap on the image so that it can be placed next to the text.

6   Save the Word file.

Your Word document should look something like this

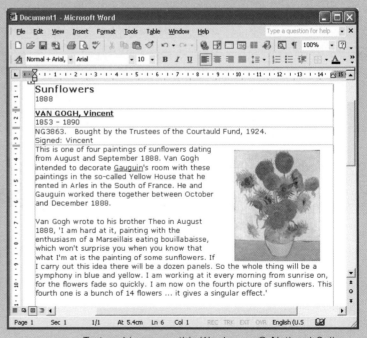

If you do not yet have a Hotmail account, sign up for one now and get your Web passport at the same time – this can be useful extra security. Start at **www.msn.com** and click the **Hotmail** link.

Text and image on this Word page © National Gallery

Searching the Web

Search engines

A search engine is a site with software that constantly scans the Web, building an indexed database of pages, which it allows visitors to search. To run a simple search in any search engine, type in one or more words to describe what you are looking for. The engine then checks through its database to find pages which contain those words in the page title, or in its headings or anywhere in the text.

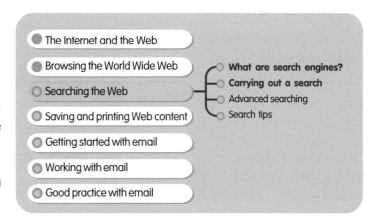

- The Internet and the Web
- Browsing the World Wide Web
  - **What are search engines?**
  - **Carrying out a search**
  - Advanced searching
  - Search tips
- Searching the Web
- Saving and printing Web content
- Getting started with email
- Working with email
- Good practice with email

Skill Builder **7.7**

1   Go to Google (**www.google.com**) and run a search for a historical event of your choice.

2   Type in a relevant name or some words to describe the event.

3   Click **Google Search**.

4   Scan through the results and click on a link to go to its page.

5   Follow up some of the resulting links, aiming to locate at least three pages containing relevant material.

6   Save one page complete with all its files.

7   From a second page, copy the headline and the first few paragraphs of text, and paste it into a new Word document. Save the file.

8   Save an image from another page.

Google is the leading search engine. It searches over 4 billion web pages, but is very fast and has a ranking system which brings to the top of the results list those that match your search closely, and have most visitors and most links from other sites.

Advanced searches

A simple search may find far too many pages – thousands or millions of them. You need to be able to focus searches.

Always be as specific as you can. For example, a search in Google for 'football' found over 40 million pages, and the top ones were all American football. The more specific 'football FA Cup' produced around 800,000 hits, and the official FA Cup site was in the first few.

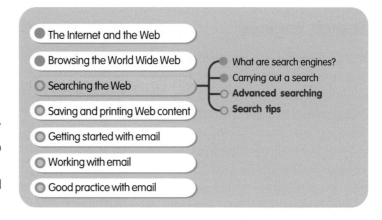

At most search engines you can run a more specific search by linking your search words with the *boolean* operators AND, OR and NOT:

> AND (or +) the following word must also be present
>
> OR match any of the linked words
>
> NOT (or –) ignore pages that contain the following word.

e.g. football AND league NOT American (or football +league -American)

This will look for pages that contain the words "football" and "league", but reject any that contain "American".

You can also write "words in quotes" (and notice that they are double quotes). This asks the engine to match the exact name or phrase.

e.g. "matrix revolutions" should find pages that relate to the film; a search on the words without the quotes, would find the film, but would also find pages on mathematics, engineering, history and much else.

You can use these operators at Google, but it also has an advanced search page. You can set up the same tight searches here, and also specify the language, file format, date and the Web domain in which to look.

 If you get no relevant results from a search, check your spelling and the way that you are using boolean operators (if you are using them).

Saving and printing Web content

Saving web page content

You can save selected text or images from web pages.

To save an image: right-click on it and select **Save Picture As...** At the **Save Picture** dialogue box, type or edit the filename and click **Save**.

In Internet Explorer 6, this toolbar appears on images – click it to save

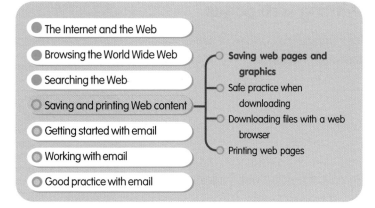

- The Internet and the Web
- Browsing the World Wide Web
- Searching the Web
- Saving and printing Web content
- Getting started with email
- Working with email
- Good practice with email
  - **Saving web pages and graphics**
  - Safe practice when downloading
  - Downloading files with a web browser
  - Printing web pages

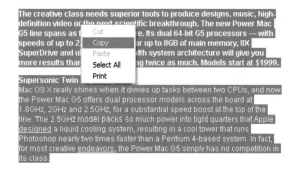

To save text: select it, right-click on it and select **Copy** then paste it into Word and save it from there.

Skill Builder 7.8

1 Go to Apple at: **www.apple.com**

2 Follow the links to find their latest, most powerful computer.

3 Copy the first two or three paragraphs of the text and paste it into Word.

4 Save the Word document, as *powermac.doc*.

5 Return to Internet Explorer. Find and save an image of the computer, as *powermac.bmp*.

In Internet Explorer 6.0, you can also save a complete page, with its images. To do this, open the **File** menu and select **Save As...** At the **Save As** dialogue box, set the **Save as** type to **Web Page complete**. The files will be saved in a subfolder with a related name – e.g. if the page is 'Mount Etna.htm', the files will be stored in 'Mount Etna_files'.

Printing web pages

You can print all or part of a web page for future reference.

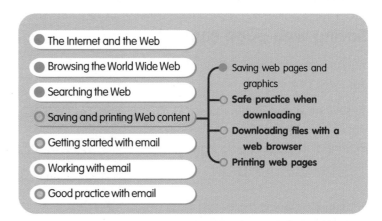

- The Internet and the Web
- Browsing the World Wide Web
- Searching the Web
  - Saving web pages and graphics
  - **Safe practice when downloading**
  - **Downloading files with a web browser**
  - **Printing web pages**
- Saving and printing Web content
- Getting started with email
- Working with email
- Good practice with email

To print the entire web page click 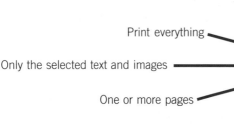.

To print part of the page:

1   Select the text and images.

2   Open the **File** menu and select **Print...**

3   In the **Print** range, click **Selection**.

4   Click **OK**.

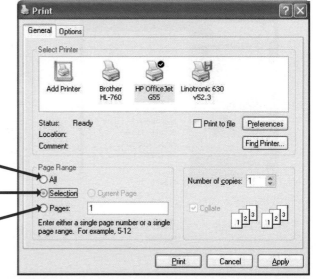

Print everything

Only the selected text and images

One or more pages

Skill Builder 7.9

1   Go to the Tate Modern gallery's site by typing in this address:

www.tate.org.uk/modern

2   Print one copy of the entire page.

3   There are pictures and text to introduce the exhibitions. Select two adjacent ones by dragging a highlight over them, then print the selected area.

Remember when downloading you should always save files so that you can check them for viruses before opening them.

 **Now try Assignment 7.1**

Getting started with email

What is email?

Email allows Internet users to send text-based files to each other. The simplest email messages use only plain text, but formatted text, images, documents, spreadsheets, and any other types of files – including viruses – can also be sent attached to messages.

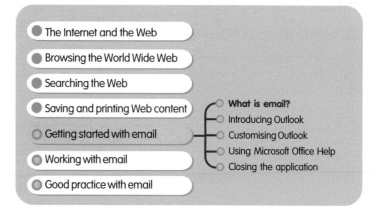

To send and receive email, you need an email account. This may be provided for you if you are at school or work. If you get online from home, an email account is normally part of the package supplied by your ISP (Internet Service Provider).

Email addresses

Addresses follow simple rules and are fairly easy to remember, but you cannot work them out for yourself and you must get them exactly right. The pattern is:

name@site.address

Notice the @ sign after the name.

The **name** is usually based on the user's real name, for example, 'Johnny B. Goode' might be allocated the names 'John_Goode', 'johnny.b.goode', 'johnnybg', 'goode123' or other variations. Underline (_) and dot (.) are often used to separate words, and a number may be added.

The **site address** is usually the same as, or based on, that of the Internet Service Provider or the organisation to which the user belongs.

You must get the address exactly right, or the message won't be delivered. The simplest way to get the address is to ask your contacts to send an email. The address will be visible in the message

Skill Builder **7.10**

1   Find the email address of three people, all using different email service providers.

2   Compare the addresses with the people's names and their providers. Do they fit the pattern?

Introducing Outlook

Microsoft Outlook can handle more than just email – it can also be used to plan your time and arrange meetings with others. However, we are only interested in its email system, so the first thing to do is configure it to focus on that.

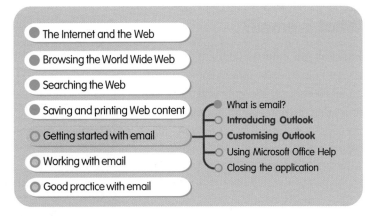

- The Internet and the Web
- Browsing the World Wide Web
- Searching the Web
- Saving and printing Web content
- Getting started with email
  - What is email?
  - **Introducing Outlook**
  - **Customising Outlook**
  - Using Microsoft Office Help
  - Closing the application
- Working with email
- Good practice with email

Skill Builder 7.11

1 Launch Outlook from the **Start** menu or desktop icon.

2 If it opens at the Outlook Today screen, click **Customize Outlook Today...** and clear the checkbox beside **When starting go directly to Outlook Today**.

3 Click **Inbox** in the Outlook bar to go to the email part of Outlook.

4 Open the **View** menu. Clear the tick beside the **Outlook bar** and tick the **Folder list** to display it – this is a better use of the screen space when working with email.

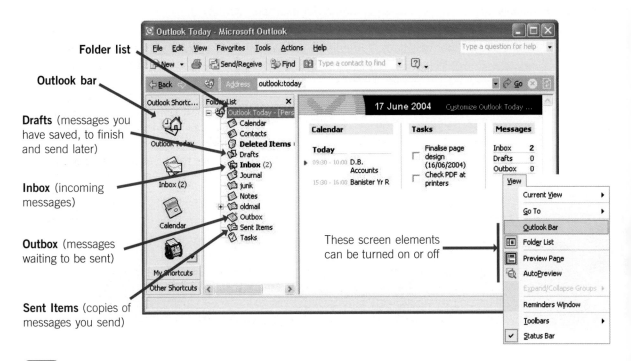

Folder list

Outlook bar

Drafts (messages you have saved, to finish and send later)

Inbox (incoming messages)

Outbox (messages waiting to be sent)

These screen elements can be turned on or off

Sent Items (copies of messages you send)

Help

Outlook is part of Microsoft Office, and so uses the same Help system.

To get specific Help, ask for it, by typing your question into the Office Assistant's bubble, or the 'Type your question here' box. When asking your question, remember that all it really needs is one or two words that describe what you want to know.

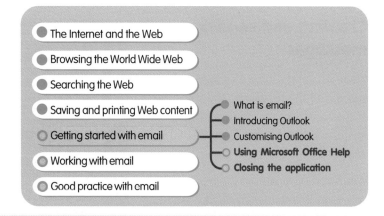

- The Internet and the Web
- Browsing the World Wide Web
- Searching the Web
- Saving and printing Web content
- Getting started with email
  - What is email?
  - Introducing Outlook
  - Customising Outlook
  - **Using Microsoft Office Help**
  - **Closing the application**
- Working with email
- Good practice with email

Skill Builder **7.12**

1 Use Help to find out how to be notified when new mail arrives.

2 Use Help to find out about AutoPreview.

To see the range of Help that is available, browse through the Contents.

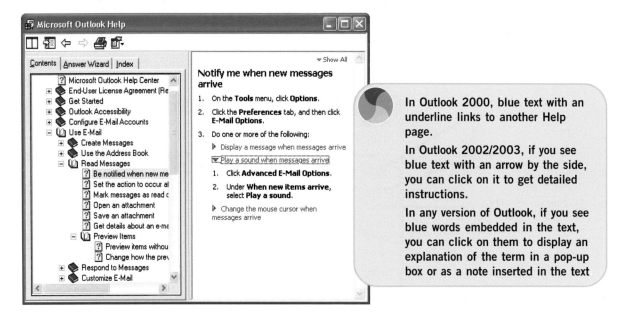

In Outlook 2000, blue text with an underline links to another Help page.

In Outlook 2002/2003, if you see blue text with an arrow by the side, you can click on it to get detailed instructions.

In any version of Outlook, if you see blue words embedded in the text, you can click on them to display an explanation of the term in a pop-up box or as a note inserted in the text

 When closing down, you will be prompted to send mail if there are messages in the Outbox. And remember that you may need to disconnect when you have done. Make sure you know how your system handles the connection.

Working with email

Creating and sending messages

When creating a new message, enter the address of the recipients and the subject of the message, then type your text – this can be edited and formatted as in Word.

When you have written the message, you can send it immediately, if you are online, or store it in the Outbox for sending when you go online.

- The Internet and the Web
- Browsing the World Wide Web
- Searching the Web
- Saving and printing Web content
- Getting started with email
- Working with email
- Good practice with email

- **Creating and sending messages**
- Reading received email
- Replying to messages
- Forwarding messages
- Editing messages
- Sending and receiving files with email
- Printing emails

Skill Builder **7.13**

1 Click New.

2 Type the recipient's address in the **To...** line.

3 Type a **Subject** – keep it brief but clear.

4 Type your message.

5 Click **Send**. The message will either be sent immediately or placed in your Outbox for mailing when you next click **Send/Receive**.

Select the format – messages can be in plain text, rich text or HTML

Click to send

Address of the main recipients

Carbon copies – people who will be sent a copy

Outline the purpose of the message so that your recipients know what's coming.

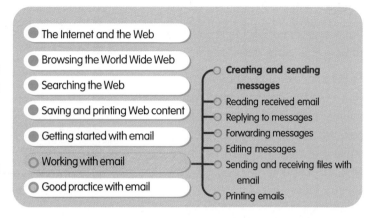

Hi Anna

Tuesday 9ᵗʰ is good for me. I can be there by 11.30.

Mac

Reading received email

Incoming messages are stored in the Inbox. The **Header pane** shows their basic details – who they are from, the subject and so on.

Clicking on a header will display its message in the **Preview pane**. Double-clicking will open a new window to display the message.

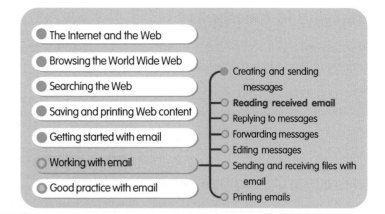

- The Internet and the Web
- Browsing the World Wide Web
- Searching the Web
- Saving and printing Web content
- Getting started with email
- Working with email
- Good practice with email

  - Creating and sending messages
  - **Reading received email**
  - Replying to messages
  - Forwarding messages
  - Editing messages
  - Sending and receiving files with email
  - Printing emails

Skill Builder 7.14

1 If the Preview pane is not present, open the **View** menu and turn it on.

2 Click **Send/Receive** to pick up your mail.

3 Select a message – if Outlook has not been used before there should be a welcome message in the Inbox.

4 Read the message in the Preview pane.

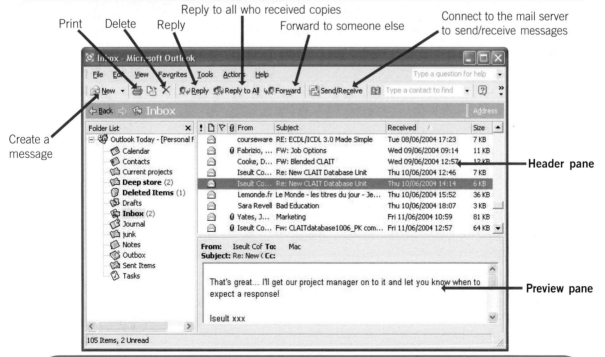

Print   Delete   Reply   Reply to all who received copies   Forward to someone else   Connect to the mail server to send/receive messages

Create a message

Header pane

Preview pane

If you have a dial-up account, email does not get delivered directly, but goes into a mailbox in the email server at your ISP. You must log in to collect it. (If you are on a local area network, the LAN software normally collects mail for everyone and distributes it.)

Replying to messages

You can reply to an incoming message, or forward it on to another person.

When you reply, the text will be copied if the **Include message in reply** option is on. It can be useful to include the original text, so that it is clear which message you are replying to. You delete any of the text you don't need.

When you forward a message, the text is always copied, of course.

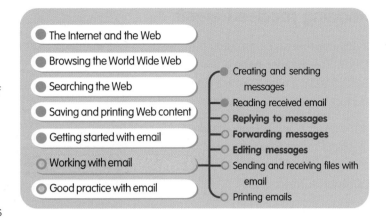

- The Internet and the Web
- Browsing the World Wide Web
- Searching the Web
- Saving and printing Web content
- Getting started with email
- Working with email
- Good practice with email
  - Creating and sending messages
  - Reading received email
  - **Replying to messages**
  - **Forwarding messages**
  - **Editing messages**
  - Sending and receiving files with email
  - Printing emails

Skill Builder **7.15**

You will need a message from a friend or colleague for this exercise.

1 Select the message.

2 Click the **Reply** toolbar button.

3 The address will have been copied into the **To** field, and the **Subject** line will now contain the original subject with 'Re:' at the start.

4 Delete any of the original text that you don't want.

5 Add your own text, before, amongst or after the original text.

6 Send the message as normal.

7 Select a second message.

8 Click the **Forward** toolbar button.

9 The **Subject** line will have been written for you, but this time you need to enter the recipient's address.

10 Edit the message or add your own text, if you want, then send as normal.

When you are replying, you can add the address to your Address Book. Right-click on the person's name or address and select Add to Contacts from the menu.

Sending and receiving files

Images, documents and other files can be sent by email, attached to messages. As the mail system was designed for transmitting plain text, these data files must be converted to text for transfer, and back again on receipt. The email software will do the conversions – all you have to do is identify the file to attach, or select a folder to store an attachment.

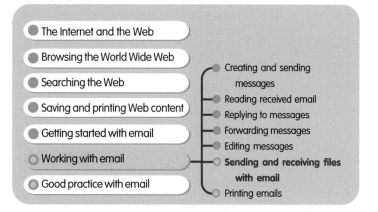

- The Internet and the Web
- Browsing the World Wide Web
- Searching the Web
- Saving and printing Web content
- Getting started with email
- Working with email
- Good practice with email
  - Creating and sending messages
  - Reading received email
  - Replying to messages
  - Forwarding messages
  - Editing messages
  - **Sending and receiving files with email**
  - Printing emails

Skill Builder 7.16

1   Start to create a new message as usual.

2   Open the **Insert** menu and select **File...** or click ⬛ ▾.

3   Locate and select the file and click **Insert**.

4   Repeat for other files, if wanted.

5   Complete and send the message.

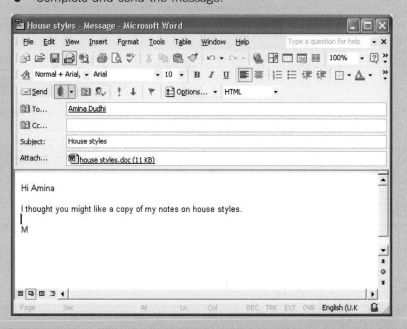

 When a file is converted for transmission, it gets about 50% bigger, and it can slow down the mail. A 1Mb photograph, for example, would be 1.5Mb as an attached file and could take up to 10 minutes to transfer on a dial-up line.

You will need to ask a friend or colleague to send you a message with an attached file to complete this exercise.

6 Select the message with the attached file.

7 Right-click on the file name in the preview pane header.

8 If you want to save the file(s), select **Save As** from the shortcut menu. In the **Save As** dialogue box, select the folder and click **Save**.

9 To open a file, select **Open.**

10 In the **Open Mail Attachment** dialogue box, select **Open it** only if you are sure it is safe, and click **OK**. The file will be opened (as long as there is a program on your computer that can handle it).

A paperclip indicates an attachment

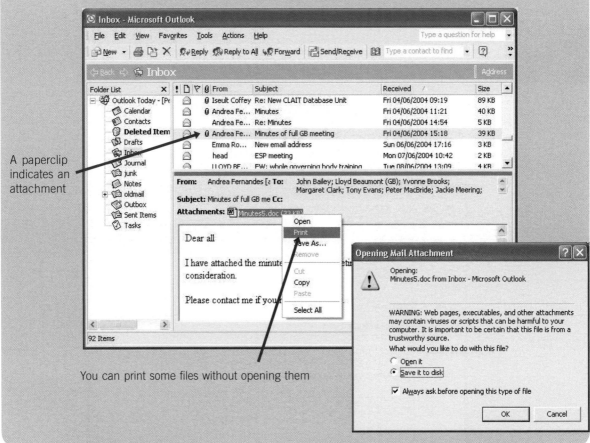

You can print some files without opening them

 Viruses can be spread as email attachments. They can be hidden in Word documents (.doc), programs (.exe, .com, .bas), screensavers (.scr) and other files that can play an active role. Never open attachments from an unknown source, and check all files for viruses, whoever has sent them.

Spell checking and printing

We all make mistakes – especially when typing email! Always spell check and proofread your messages before sending them. Mistakes can mislead.

Printing

You can print a message when you are reading or writing it, or after selecting it from the Header pane in the main display. Just click the 🖨 **Print** button.

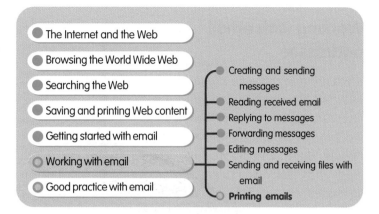

- The Internet and the Web
- Browsing the World Wide Web
- Searching the Web
- Saving and printing Web content
- Getting started with email
- Working with email
- Good practice with email
  - Creating and sending messages
  - Reading received email
  - Replying to messages
  - Forwarding messages
  - Editing messages
  - Sending and receiving files with email
  - **Printing emails**

Skill Builder 7.17

1 Type the following message quickly, without watching the keyboard too closely! We want some mistakes.

The committee has decided that the school needed separate accommodation for the new classes in gymnastics. These will start in September provided that suitable teachers can be found.

2 Click the ᴬᴮꟲ **Spell check** button and run a check.

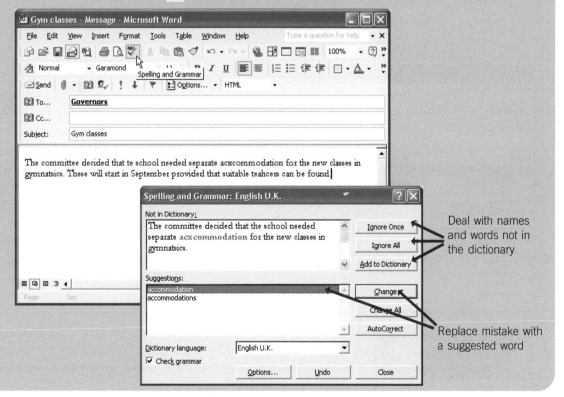

Good practice with email

Working with email addresses

If you are going to write to someone, you must have their email address – and if you are going to write to them often, you should keep the address in your Address Book. This can hold not only email addresses, but also postal addresses, phone numbers and other details.

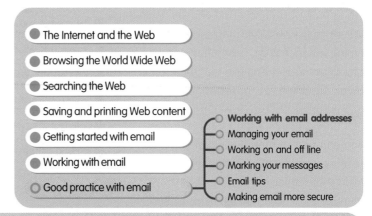

- ● The Internet and the Web
- ● Browsing the World Wide Web
- ● Searching the Web
- ● Saving and printing Web content
- ● Getting started with email
- ● Working with email
- ● Good practice with email
  - ○ **Working with email addresses**
  - ○ Managing your email
  - ○ Working on and off line
  - ○ Marking your messages
  - ○ Email tips
  - ○ Making email more secure

Skill Builder **7.18**

1 Open the **Tools** menu and select **Address Book...** or click 📖 .

2 At the **Address Book**, open the **File** menu and select **New Entry...** or click the **New** button and select **New Contact**...

3 On the **General** tab type the person's name. You can enter it directly into the **Full Name** field, or click its button to enter the details.

4 Type the address into the **E-mail** field.

5 Go to the other tabs to add further details.

6 Click **Save and Close**.

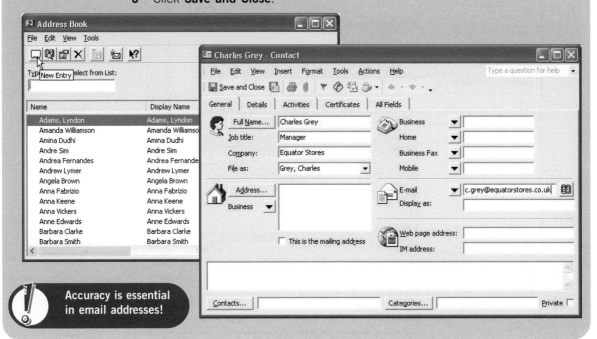

Accuracy is essential in email addresses!

Managing your email

The Inbox can soon get crowded. Keep yours under control by deleting unwanted messages, and by creating – and using – your own folders to store messages for future reference.

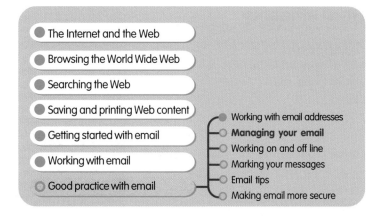

- The Internet and the Web
- Browsing the World Wide Web
- Searching the Web
- Saving and printing Web content
- Getting started with email
- Working with email
- Good practice with email
  - Working with email addresses
  - **Managing your email**
  - Working on and off line
  - Marking your messages
  - Email tips
  - Making email more secure

Skill Builder **7.19**

1   Open the **File** menu, point to **New** and select **Folder**.

2   At the **Create New Folder** dialogue box, enter the name *Oldmail* and select the top level of the folder list to position it. Click **OK**.

3   Go through the messages in your Inbox.

4   Delete those that are no longer wanted.

5   Move those you want to keep to the *Oldmail* folder.

New folder name

Where the folder will be created

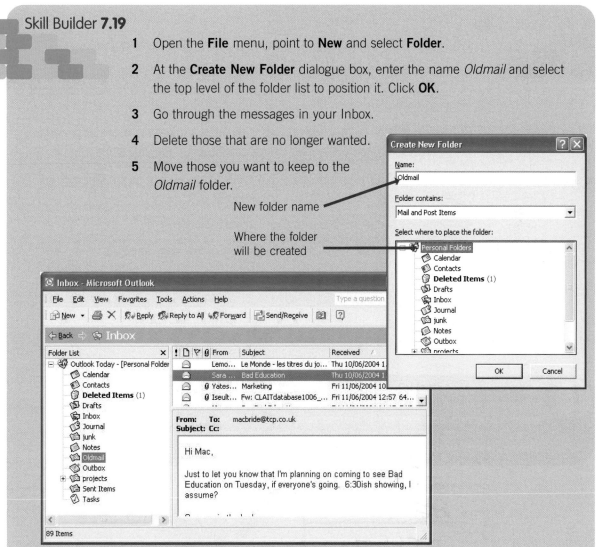

Email efficiency

Try to develop the right working habits so that your emailing can be effective, efficient and safe.

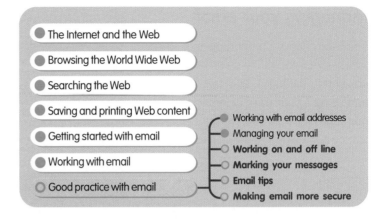

- The Internet and the Web
- Browsing the World Wide Web
- Searching the Web
- Saving and printing Web content
- Getting started with email
- Working with email
- Good practice with email
  - Working with email addresses
  - Managing your email
  - **Working on and off line**
  - **Marking your messages**
  - **Email tips**
  - **Making email more secure**

Skill Builder **7.20**

1 Open the **Options** dialogue box and go to the **Mail Delivery** tab.

2 Set the **Send immediately...** option so that it best suits your way of working – if you only go online for as long as it takes to send and receive messages, it should be off.

3 Set the **Check for new messages...** option to a suitable level. Every check slows down other online work – how often do you need to do it?

You will need the co-operation of a friend or colleague for the next part of this exercise.

4 Compose a new message to your exercise partner.

5 Flag the message for reply, setting a date a few days ahead.

6 Send the message.

7 When you receive your partner's message, reply to it, and set its flag to complete.

> Virus alert! Handle email with care. Do not open any attachment without checking it for viruses. And if someone sends you a warning about a new virus and asks you to tell everyone you know about it, don't do it! This will just clog up the email delivery system and other people's Inboxes, which means that the message is itself a kind of virus.

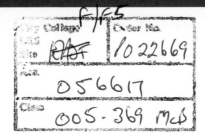

Now try Assignment 7.2